LOVE
HANDLES

PASTORS BRIAN & JESSI GIBSON

ISBN 979-8-9864278-4-3

Copyright 2021 by Pastors Brian & Jessi Gibson

Thrive Publishing

Published by Thrive Publishing

3920 W 91st St

Tulsa, Oklahoma 74132

CONTENTS

ENDORSEMENTS

"Brian and Jessi Gibson are a power couple with a message that our culture desperately needs to hear right now. This book will refresh your marriage, strengthen your faith, and set you up for success as you seek God's original intent for married life. I highly recommend this book!"

DR. CHÉ AHN

Senior Pastor, Harvest Rock Church, Pasadena, CA
President, Harvest International Ministry
International Chancellor, Wagner University

"Loving each other, raising kids, serving and honoring God are the pillars of Brian and Jessi's marriage. No matter what they face, they face it together and become stronger through it all. Their standards of love and perseverance are as high as they can be, it's actually been great watching them navigate the adventures of their lives."

PASTOR BILL SCHEER

Guts Church | Tulsa, Oklahoma

"For years, Brian and Jessi Gibson have conducted marriage seminars that have not only strengthened marriages, but have healed and helped couples stay together. This couple presents in this book, not only a spiritual, but common sense approach for your marriage to have excitement and enthusiasm."

DR. BOB RODGERS

Evangel World Prayer Center | Louisville, Ky

"Brian and Jessi Gibson are successful pastors, but more than that they are successful in life which is reflected in their marriage and their family. Their story and the insights they have learned and share in this book will inspire you to make your marriage all it can be. As I read their book I found myself wanting to do a better job at loving my wife and family and you will do the same."

DR. JAMES MAROCCO

Global Senior Pastor | King's Cathedral and Chapels

INTRODUCTION

"It was a late May evening in West Texas in 1998. Teenagers were hopping from school to school and house party to house party all over town."

It was graduation night for the high schools and my friends and I were going to attend every fun event we could possibly find. We had a plan to stay up all night and we made my parents house our rally point. I had no interest in wasting my time on boys in my Junior year. Many of my friends had gotten distracted and found themselves in trouble. That was not going to be me. In fact, I had decided that I would ignore them completely until after high school. I enjoyed my friends and had a really strong youth group that kept me busy every spare minute that I wasn't playing volleyball.

I was in love with God and completely committed to living for Him. I was young and naive. I was happy and healthy. I had no idea what was about to take place but God was about to give me exactly what I needed in a package that I couldn't resist. I walked into my parents house for a quick wardrobe change and right in front of me stood a young cowboy I had never met. He had manners and blue eyes. I was oblivious at the time but that would later prove to be a lethal combination. Little did I know that God was giving me an opportunity to love and be loved. That man would turn out to be my best friend. I would choose to love him. I would forever be in a competition to love him better than he loved me. I had a lot to learn."

-Pastor Jessi Gibson

"LOVE HANDLES - LET'S TALK ABOUT THEM. IN A WORLD THAT WANTS TO PHOTOSHOP EVERYTHING AWAY, I THINK THEY NEED ATTENTION MORE NOW THAN EVER!"

I know what you're thinking, "Why would I want to talk about the misshapen, side fat that plagues me?" You have a good point! But think about the pros involved with love handles. OK, honestly I can't think of many, except one - they are great to grab ahold of! Although some of us have more of them than we would like (why are the carbs always so good?), we all have them!

My wife, Jessi and I have been married since 2000. We knew each other for about two years before we married. It sounds crazy, but I knew I would marry Jessi the first time I laid eyes on her. Unfortunately, she didn't have the same "love at first sight" thing going as me. I can't say I blame her, I was a work in progress. But I started working on myself spiritually, emotionally, relationally, and physically. I wasn't just working for Jessi. I had recently met Jesus. More than anything else, I wanted to live a life that would honor God. I promise you this; if you will honor God, He will honor you! Once I took that step, he began to change me in more ways than I can list.

During this time of my life, I decided that I would get back in shape. I had done several years of hard-partying and It really had taken its toll. I wanted a completely new me. I went on a low-carb diet and didn't touch a carb for at least a year before we married. The fat melted off my body and I hit the gym every day. I looked like a different person. As a matter of fact, the last time I can remember not having love handles was at our wedding. It seems the moment I said "I do," the love handles jumped back on. The way I see it, it's more for Jessi to love. She's a lucky girl!

You don't live with someone for over two decades without learning how to aggravate them (in a loving way of course). Jessi loves to grab my love handles because she knows I hate it. If you're walking side-by-side with your arm around your spouse, your hand will naturally rest on that love handle. That's the origin of the name. It is something to grab ahold of. A handle for your love. In some sense that's what the American marriage scene is missing. It's like we've lost a handle on what love actually is. Many people don't know what to grab ahold of anymore. We desperately need eternal truths to hold onto.

People want something to hold onto. No one wants a marriage that doesn't work. No one wants to go through the emotional pain of a divorce. I believe that often people haven't seen a relationship model that they can grab onto and apply to their own life.

We used to work with a ministry that would bus kids into a church service from a poverty stricken neighborhood. The ministry would bring them to a safe place, feed them and show them the love of Jesus. The man that ran this ministry told us that he loved having husband and wife teams working with the kids because most of them had never seen a marriage that worked.

I remember one time a little boy asked me if Jessi was my girlfriend. I answered him, "No, she's my wife." He answered back, "You mean she is staying with you." The boy had no concept of a man and woman who were married or could possibly stay that way "till death do us part". He had no model to hold onto. He had no love handle. I'll never forget us trying to explain to him what marriage really was."

- Pastor Brian Gibson

DON'T LET GO

"Over the years we have had the privilege of ministering to many young students."

A large percentage of young people have never had the luxury of viewing a healthy marriage relationship. Many times they grew up missing a parent or going between two homes in order to keep a relationship with both. If, at some point, both parents were in the home, they may have dealt with deafening silence or loud disagreement. They typically haven't seen people fight and then repent for what they said or did to hurt the one they are in a relationship with. They have only seen the fights end in abuse or the end of a marriage. We have had multiple young people tell us that it made them nervous when we disagreed.

They would tell us that a disagreement over which direction to go on a road trip would have ended differently in their home. These same young people would then see that some disagreements turn into agreement and even a laugh or two. This reportedly "changed their view on marriage". Many of those same people are married and leading families with strength, and love for Jesus. One view into something healthy gave them hope for a future that would last. It is vitally important in this day and age that we get around people with healthy relationships and take the time to study them. This is the kind of hope found in God's word that we can enter into a covenant and then stay in that covenant for life. However, both parties must be willing to participate in the education and participation.

A few years ago, I was on a float trip on a rapids course in Tennessee. I had a friend as my seat buddy. I had specifically chosen her because she was strong. I was a little nervous about the trip because I am not a strong swimmer. I felt like she would be helpful and not put me at any further risk. It wasn't until after I was in the raft that I realized my mistake. She was not willing, or able, to hold on. She was also double my size. So, this turned into two hours of us hitting rapids and her body slamming me into the tumultuous water. I could not withstand the hit without flying out of the boat. I got caught under the boat and almost drowned at one point and when I returned to the boat she giggled and did not take it seriously. I realized at this moment how vital it is to know that your partner is not only able, but willing to hold on.

Check your own heart today and ask yourself a question; Am I willing to hold on? God has given you the capability, but you must search your heart and decide whether or not you are willing to hold on and not let go of the promises God has for your marriage. No one wants a spouse that shrugs their shoulders and giggles when danger is present.

Everyone needs a spouse that will do whatever it takes to stay and keep you safe in the boat with them. The easiest way to start this in your marriage is to become that spouse.

The God of the Bible is called the God of Jacob. Jacob is an interesting man in scripture. He wasn't always upright as a person. He tricked his brother out of his birthright, and stole his brother's blessing through treachery. Jacob was a bit of a shady character until he grabbed hold of our gracious God.

The Angel of the Lord, or some manifestation of God , appeared to Jacob (Genesis 32). Jacob wrestled with God and stated that he would not let go unless God blessed him. That's crazy faith - I won't let go unless I am blessed by God. Jacob's name was changed that night to Israel. He received His blessing and the rest is history. If you want a marriage that lasts - hold on!!!!!

- Pastor Jessi Gibson

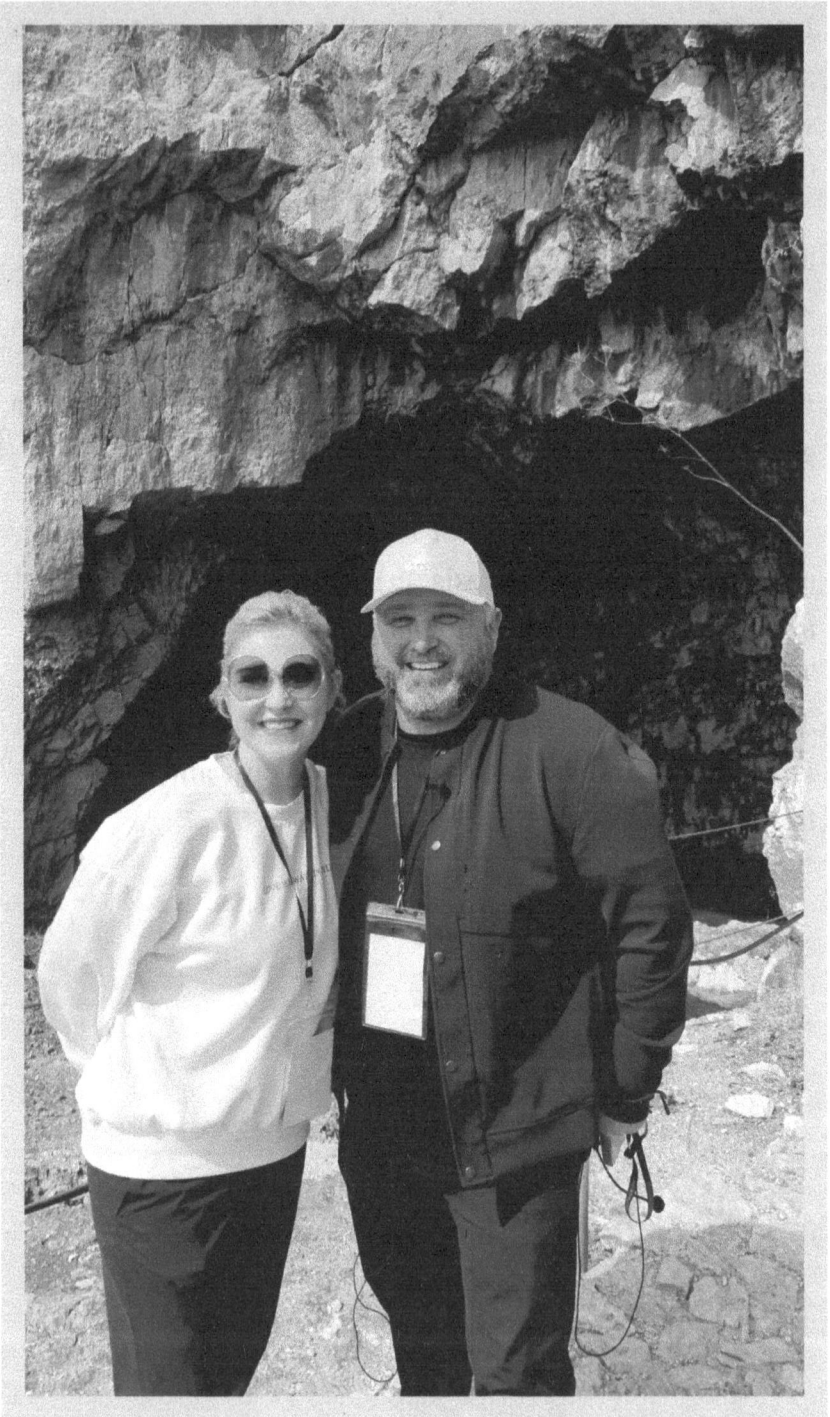

CHAPTER 1:

LOVE HANDLES LONELINESS

"And the LORD God said, "It is not good that man should be alone; I will make him a helper comparable to him." Out of the ground the LORD God formed every beast of the field and every bird of the air, and brought them to Adam to see what he would call them. And whatever Adam called each living creature, that was its name. So Adam gave names to all cattle, to the birds of the air, and to every beast of the field. But for Adam there was not found a helper comparable to him. And the LORD God caused a deep sleep to fall on Adam, and he slept; and He took one of his ribs, and closed up the flesh in its place. Then the rib which the LORD God had taken from man He made into a woman, and He brought her to the man. And Adam said: "This is now bone of my bones And flesh of my flesh; She shall be called Woman, Because she was taken out of Man." Therefore a man shall leave his father and mother and be joined to his wife, and they shall become one flesh. And they were both naked, the man and his wife, and were not ashamed."
Genesis 2:18-25 NKJV

"IF THERE'S ONE THING I WANT YOU TO WALK AWAY FROM THIS BOOK KNOWING, IT'S THAT GOD IS FOR YOUR MARRIAGE."

I want you to say this out loud; <u>God is for my marriage!</u> Say it one more time; <u>God is for my marriage!</u> There's great strength in knowing that. You see, marriage wasn't something that was invented by man, marriage is something that was ordained by God. There is a law that Bible scholars teach about Theology (the study of God) called "The law of first mention."

"The law of first mention" states that whenever a topic is first mentioned in the Bible, there is massive truth revealed about the topic. Marriage isn't just something that's mentioned in the Bible. It's one of the first topics that's covered in the first book of the Bible!

> "And the LORD God said, "It is not good that man should be alone; I will make him a helper comparable to him." Genesis 2:18 NKJV

16

The Bible records that God made the first man, Adam, out of dust from the ground. He picked Adam up. Can you imagine seeing God pick up the lifeless body of the first man? God then takes Adam into His hands and the scripture says that He breathed into Adam the breath of life. This is what caused man to become a living being. This is what makes us different from any other creature on the earth – the breath of God. God then gives Adam a job, he is to tend and keep the garden. Adam is placed in a perfect paradise.

Can you imagine the beauty of the world that had not yet fallen? This was the only world that Adam knew at this point. God Himself would come down and walk with Adam in the cool of the day. God and man walked together in the garden! Even though Adam had a purpose; even though Adam had a perfect environment, and even though Adam had a relationship with God Himself, there was still something missing. The Scripture says it all, "It is not good that man should be alone."

-Pastor Brian Gibson

IT CERTAINLY WASN'T GOOD WHEN I WAS ALONE

"YOU CAN LOOK AT THE SHAPE OF MOST MEN'S BACHELOR PADS AND YOU'LL KNOW THAT IT IS NOT GOOD FOR THE MAN TO BE ALONE! THAT WAS CERTAINLY TRUE OF MY PLACE!"

As a young man, I had done a fantastic job of messing up my life. Before I graduated high school I had already delved into a life of drug use and binge drinking. In the 90's, methamphetamine arrived to the scene strong in the in my small town of Providence, Kentucky. Meth had me at hello. It ruled my life from my senior year of high school until just about a month before my twenty-first birthday. I was addicted and broken.

Then something happened in my life. My brother who I used to party with started going to church. His life drastically changed! He started talking to me about Jesus and how I could live a life of purpose. To tell you the truth, it drove me crazy when his life took a turn for the better. I'd lost my party buddy. Who in the world was I going to drink and drug with now?

I did almost everything I could to make him stumble in his new relationship with Jesus. I would go to his house with a bottle of Maker's Mark and try to get him drunk with me. I would wave bags of cocaine in his face and try to get him to get high. I even went as far as making fun of his Pastor, be careful who you make fun of. The irony of God is that he took me and made me what I used to make fun of! Finally, his prayers, and the prayers of other family members, began to pay off. I had an encounter with Jesus. I repented of my sins and asked him to come into my life.

My brother set up a golf trip with his family for me to go on. When I say set up I mean a setup! The kicker was that a Pastor was going to be on the trip and that Pastor happened to be my future Father-in-Law. It was one of the first weeks that I had lived drug-free in many years. It wasn't easy but I made it through the week. At the end of the week, it was time to go home. To give myself a few more weeks of sobriety before I went around my old stomping ground, Pastor David came to me and asked me if I would like to go to his home in Amarillo, Texas. He had a pretty daughter so I went! I spent a couple of weeks in Amarillo and decided to move there to give God space to work in my life.

God moved in my life over the course of the next two years in a massive way. I became a completely new creation, I learned to live free from my addictions, and I learned to have a social life that wasn't built around alcohol. The word of God grew in my heart. It was a process that lasted for about two years. During this process, Jessi and I became best friends! I loved her with all of my heart and didn't know how to tell her. Jesus had made me whole but I was still alone in the natural sense. I wanted a wife!"

– *Pastor Brian Gibson*

YOU WERE CREATED FOR COMPANIONSHIP!

God caused a deep sleep to fall upon Adam. After Adam fell asleep God came down and opened the side of the first man. The Bible records that God took a rib from the side of Adam. He just might have opened his love handle (humor me for the sake of the title of this book). Then, God began to craft the greatest thing that Adam had ever seen, he finely handcrafted Eve. When Adam names her he said Wooooooooo man! Thus the name, woman.

Adam had a desire in his heart that was fulfilled in Eve. He now had another person to share life with. They could fulfill their purpose, together. They could start a family together. They could enjoy fellowship with God the Father, together.

It doesn't matter if you are an introvert or an extrovert, you have a need for community. The marriage relationship fulfills that need at the deepest level possible. Mankind is made in the image of God and this makes us different from any other species. We have this God likeness about us. God Himself dwells in community. He is a Trinity. Completely One, yet three distinct personalities in one. God Himself is a relational God. If we are made in His image, then we are made to be relational as well.

Marriage is the deepest form of companionship. It's created to bring comfort, friendship, love, help, assistance, and a strength that holds on, even when you are not strong enough on your own. Two are so much better than one. The benefits outweigh the costs when marriage is seen properly and handled with care.

Marriage is durable and it can stand the test of time but it was never meant to be used and abused. It was not created to be taken lightly and thrown around without care or concern. It is precious and priceless and is to be handled with gentleness and adoration.

COMPANIONSHIP COSTS SOMETHING.

"Often people are happy to make the initial investment of a rib for a marriage."

New buyers are extremely excited. They are happy to get fixed up, to put their best foot forward in the dating relationship, even to sacrifice financially for the wedding of their dreams. But for some reason, after the I do's, they're not so happy about continuing to invest. It's almost like the new car buyer. They can almost smell that new car smell. They are so excited about getting that new, shiny, vehicle of their dreams! They have visions of cruising in their new ride, but they are not excited about maintaining and insuring their new vehicle.

I was incredibly excited to get married at the very tender age of 19. As soon as Brian asked me to marry him I began to tell my friends and family. I noticed that their response was simply "Congratulations" or "Have you thought about..." usually followed by something I was going to need to give up in order to be married. People see a very young girl making a decision for life and they feel compelled to warn her, I get it and I appreciated the concern. However, I thought that there was nothing I wasn't willing to sacrifice to be married to Brian. Well, I was mistaken. I had dreams of traveling the world and preaching the gospel but when my lack of availability to do so once I was married was brought up, I quickly panicked. I remember feeling trapped. I wanted out of the engagement. Not because I didn't want to be married but because I thought it would cost me something near and dear to my heart. I went to talk to Brian, he asked me a few questions and then he said "Would it be OK if I came too?" Wow, I hadn't thought of that, I was used to making decisions based on what I wanted. I would need to adjust the plan but it wasn't necessary to scrap it! Brian could be with me on every adventure. We would both need to sacrifice but there was a way forward that protected dreams and provided companionship.

I think it's important to notice that Adam had to give something up to get something greater in return. There is an eternal law that is in the earth called sowing and reaping. As humans, we have to plant a seed, to get a harvest. Adam had to sow a costly seed of a rib to get the harvest of Eve! A God-honoring marriage is the answer to the loneliness problem! Anything worth having in life will inevitably cost you something and this is also true with marriage."

-Pastor Jessi Gibson

"I REMEMBER AFTER I ASKED JESSI TO MARRY ME I FOUND OUT THAT WE HAD TO GO THROUGH PREMARITAL COUNSELING."

I had never considered having to do such a thing. I was always taught to keep my cards very close to me – opening up to some sort of counselor wasn't my thing. But to get the girl you have to play by the rules so I relented and went. The Pastor that did our premarital counseling said this to me, "You're about to enter into a fiery baptism! You don't know how much this is going to cost you!" He went out of his way to tell me that marriage would be great but that it would also cost me something. He was right, marriage cost Adam a rib. If you want a love that will handle the loneliness that life can dish out, I promise you will need to invest.

Going back to the new car buyer Jessi mentioned; most new car buyers are excited about the new car, but when they're asked to fork out the down payment, it's not as fun because you now have to start to invest in it. Fast forward a few years and you'll see that this initial investment will continued to grow. That new car smell is long gone and this car has now been lived in! Kids have now eaten happy meals in the vehicle and it smells like they hid a milk box under the seat somewhere three months ago. The shine isn't the same.

If you want to keep the car new, you need to continue to invest in it. You have to have it detailed so to speak. You have to perform regular maintenance on the vehicle, change the oil, check the fluids, and put gas in the tank. **If you want a marriage to remain new you will have to continually invest in its upkeep.**

If you want to find a way to keep the spark alive, invest in your relationship and invest in your spouse. You are going to live a life with this person, so you should do everything in your power to ensure that they are a well watered garden. Don't just do marriage, continue to date your spouse. It's amazing how far small investments into each other will go if you make them on a continual basis. I also promise that the more you invest in your relationship, the more you will reap back from the relationship.

After twenty years of marriage, one thing that has amazed me over and over again is the fact that the small things and attention to detail are some of the most impactful investments.

— Pastor Brian Gibson

"We had a friend that absolutely loved coffee. Coffee was comforting to her and she really felt loved when someone would take the time to bring her a cup."

Her husband knew this but he saw it as an ignorant thing that shouldn't make a difference. He was a little cheap by nature and thought that a latte was just a selfish waste of the family's monthly budget. This wife saw it as something that made her feel special and valued.

Over the course of their twenty-two year marriage he abused her verbally, he treated her terribly, he never took her on dates without complaining about the expense of the date. Even on their anniversaries, he would try to talk her into cheaper food and complain if she wanted to go somewhere special or even catch a movie. He would say things like "You're spoiled" or "Nothing I do is ever good enough." In all reality, she was happy with pretty much anything he did as long as it was his idea and he tried.

He refused to help with anything even though she worked full time. He spoke evil of her to others, demanded a lot, and invested almost nothing. From the outside looking in,

I could see the unhappiness, abuse, and hatred that grew in their home. Finally, things took a turn for the worse and she became afraid for her safety and the safety of her children.

She immediately told him to leave the house and not return. I understood her concern, supported her decision, and thought that this major outburst was simply the straw that broke the marriage's back. He begged to return home. He missed his children and wanted everything to return to normal, but normal was nothing she was interested in. She was solemn but not emotional. I hadn't fully understood that she had been closing her heart for years and it had finally snapped shut for the very last time.

Honestly, it wasn't until a few weeks later that I saw the emotion rise in this young lady. It was a busy day and her estranged husband asked if he could come over to the house. When he arrived he was there with a coffee in his hand, a coffee for her. It was exactly what she liked. It was hot and wonderful. He was so proud of his "move." When she saw it, her emotions ran hot. She began to weep painful tears. She called me and wept uncontrollably. She was inconsolable.

Once I got her to settle down enough to speak I asked her what on earth had upset her so badly. I figured he yelled and called her names or worse yet had hit her again or hurt her physically in some other way. I found myself stunned at her response, "He brought me coffee. I cannot believe he brought me coffee!" I asked her why coffee would make her so angry. She responded, "In twenty-two years he has never brought me coffee. He's brought everyone else coffee and seemed to enjoy the fact that I didn't get one. He never once brought one to me, now I realize, he knew what I liked the whole time and refused to love me!" This small act was huge to her. Knowing that he knew but didn't care enough about her to show her the affection that she desired so deeply was devastating. It broke her heart and set off a course of mourning that I have rarely seen in my twenty years of ministry experience. The little things matter.

The investment of time and attention is important. The care of details is a game-changer. Don't wait to invest until it is too late. Be proactive, and whatever you do, show love in a way that your spouse knows it's personal.

It may not make you look impressive to others. No one else in the room may even know that you are investing, but if it translates to your spouse, that's all that matters."

—Pastor Jessi Gibson

"Brian and I have very specific things that we have learned about each other in the last twenty years."

Some of those are things that bother each other, and some are things that our spouse really enjoys. When Brian does things that I love with no backlash or complaint, it is extremely touching and makes me feel loved. He knows when he has done it and I know as well. No one else in the room may even recognize that anything changed, but we know.

Most of the time that I have spent helping couples one on one has been focused on small things. It's almost never the major things in life that break the relationship. It is usually a spouse that refuses to be intentional about the small things that sets off a big marriage moment.

Next time you decide to show a gesture of romance I encourage you to think about what your spouse loves. Then do your best to do it as many times as you can in a week. See what kind of strides you can make relationally by paying attention to the small things.

A lot of times, people inside a marriage will simply do things they have seen in movies. While others may feel pressure to buy gifts or take their spouse on a trip that they don't know how they will ever pay for. This does not have to be the way. Those things may work because they suit your spouse but maybe you are doing those things and getting nowhere. It may be time to invest attention and genuinely try to find something that only matters to the person you love. It may be small, private, personal, or simple, but that's not just okay, that is wonderful. It is a good investment."

—Pastor Jessi Gibson

TIPS ON INVESTMENT

"I'LL NEVER FORGET WHEN I OPENED MY FIRST BANK ACCOUNT AS A YOUNG MAN."

The first account was a savings account that my family set up for me. I can remember my mother talking to me about savings and putting some money that I had from a birthday into the account. This account was to be used for college in the future. Once it was opened, I went to the bank with Mom, and then I never really heard about it again. The money went into the account and that was it.

When I turned about twelve years old it was time for me to start working for my father's business. I had already been working for several years at this point but I was going to start getting paid. My parents had more work than they knew what to do with. Dad was a broker of feeder cattle, and thousands of cattle would arrive at my family farm to be processed and shipped out daily. It was great training ground on hard work for a young man and I'm thankful that my family put me to work early in life. Every day after school (except in football season) I would head to the livestock to work till almost 10:00 pm. I'll never forget when I received my first paycheck. I was so excited. Mom took me to the bank to set up a checking account. I learned that my paycheck would go into the account and that I had the power to make withdrawals.

DEPOSITS AND WITHDRAWALS

"I REMEMBER SPENDING MORE THAN I DEPOSITED IN MY ACCOUNT WHEN I TURNED ABOUT SIXTEEN YEARS OLD. MY OLDER BROTHER, BEN, WENT WITH ME TO THE BANK TO STRAIGHTEN IT OUT."

He looked me in the eye and scolded me, "You can't cash checks when you haven't deposited enough money - you can't expect the bank to just float you!" I'll never forget his words.

There are a lot of people that need my brother's advice in their lives and especially in their marriages. You can't cash checks when you haven't made enough deposits! How much have you been depositing into your marriage? How much have you been withdrawing? What is the balance on the account? I want to encourage you to be honest with yourself.

STOP EXPECTING YOUR SPOUSE TO JUST FLOAT YOU!

I see so many people trying to make withdrawals from their spouse. They want a withdrawal of affections, sex, companionship, or praise. When they find their account empty they are often angry at their spouse. Then they start questioning the spouse. How do they not understand my needs? Do they not care?

The truth is, they often do care, they're just empty. The balance is negative and they can't find the emotional currency to spend on the relationship anymore. They feel alone again because no one has been investing. When you don't sow you don't reap.

Jessi and I have given our lives to Pastoring people. It's our great purpose and calling. We have always loved ministering to others, but while we attended school in Tulsa, Oklahoma we began to feel that we were called to start a church. We planted a church from scratch in Owensboro, Kentucky in 2004. We didn't know anyone from the town but felt the Lord leading us there after a time of prayer and fasting. I must admit that I probably underestimated the time and energy it would take to start a church. In those early years, we had few resources but we made up for it with work ethic.

Jessi and I worked together almost around the clock for several years. We were together all day long, we started early and ended our days late - together. I thought that everything was fine with our marriage, no one spent as much time together as we did and I mean no one. One night Jessi came to me and told me that we needed to talk. I had overdrawn our account. She said that she needed more than a working relationship. She needed some time and romance in life, and she was right. I had made a crucial mistake, I had overdrawn the account.

I thought that time together was all that mattered. There is a difference between time together and real-time together. There is a difference between quantity and quality! I had been in the room with her but she had felt alone. We talked it out and decided that we would become systematic about investing in our marriage so we scheduled a date night on our calendar. We made Thursday night a sacred space for our relationship because it was the night we would invest in one another!

PLAN YOUR INVESTMENTS!

Good investing isn't just a shot in the dark. God had a plan to remove the rib of Adam and create Eve! I doubt that God just knocked Adam out and figured it out from there! Well, should I take his right hand, or how about his toes, or maybe a vertebrae? No, God had a plan. It would cost Adam a rib.

Jessi gave me some incredible advice back in those days - she told me how she honestly felt. She told me that our romantic life needed to be planned! She wanted a place on my schedule and it needed to be consistent. What gets put on the calendar gets completed in real life, and what we intend to get to someday gets ignored. I can not afford to ignore the most important relationship in my life. It must be planned."

-Pastor Brian Gibson

"We knew a couple that we sought advice and mentorship from years ago. They taught us a valuable marriage principle back in those days. They called the principle "The Law of Seven."

- They taught us to have a date at least every seven days.
- They taught us to have a night without the kids every seven weeks.
- They taught us to find a way to take a short vacation with each other every seven months.
- We added this one - tell them you love them and invest verbally every seven hours.

Some of you are thinking, "I can't afford a date like that" or "We can barely make ends meet, how can I go on a vacation?" Listen, the point isn't the money spent, the point is the time spent. If all you can do is get a soda and a burger together - do it! Time spent doesn't have to be flowers and expensive gifts, to be a real connection.

One of the sweetest things Brian ever gave me was a wildflower that he got one day while he was working on the tractor in the middle of a field. By the time he got home, it was wilted from being inside the cab with him in the hot sun all day. He apologized that it wasn't prettier, but explained it was all by itself in a field and he was thinking of me so he decided to stop the tractor, hop out, and pick it. It cost him nothing except time and attention but that nothing turned into a lot. It meant the world to me. I felt so loved. I told him not to apologize. It was better than anything he had ever paid for and given me as a gift and is still my favorite thing he has ever given to me.

We are all looking for a connection deep in our hearts and all need to know we are loved, but to receive real connections you must plan times for communication. Without times of communication, you will most likely never know what makes your spouse tick. Love takes attention and growing, meaning that love requires effort and time. I have heard so many people say, "I just feel like if they are the one for you it should be easy!" Nothing could be further from the truth. **No matter how much you mean to each other, time and intentionality will grow love. Without these things, you will not experience the growth of relational intimacy."**

—Pastor Jessi Gibson

LOVE HANDLE:

Make it a priority today to set up a Law of Seven Schedule with your spouse.

CHAPTER 2:

LOVE HANDLES PROTECTION

"So the husbands ought to love their own wives as their own bodies; he who loves his wife loves himself. For no one ever hated his own flesh, but nourishes and cherishes it, just as the Lord does the church." EPHESIANS 5:28-29 NKJV

"In the nearly two decades that Brian and I have been married, we have traveled often."

Whether we were on the road in a car going from church to church ministering, visiting family that lived hundreds of miles away, enjoying a much-needed vacation, or flying from campus to campus building churches, we have traveled enough to create systems. Truth be told, we don't even talk about it, we just do what we've known and it works for us.

There is no conversation about who will park the car while the other goes in to check us into a flight or deciding who holds the baby and who folds the stroller at the TSA check. We know exactly who takes the children in to get snacks, and who fills the car with gas. Goodness knows that there is no discussing who packs the suitcases while the other one keeps the children from destroying the latest packed bag. We have a system, we know each other, and we have roles that we play.

Any distraction from this system seems loud. The smallest detour can feel like an earthquake among us. We have also been in such close proximity to one another for so many years that even a change in voice tone triggers attention.

This is exactly what took place one fateful day in the St. Louis airport. As usual, Brian was quickly walking several feet in front of me as he rushed down the terminal to get to our tight connection. Not far behind him, I was approached by a very large man who quickly moved in to talk with me.

He proceeded to tell me that I smelled amazing and was wondering if I could tell him what the name of my perfume was. I started walking a little quicker but he refused to move away. He stepped in front of me and stopped me dead in my tracks. He then moved in to smell my neck and I couldn't believe it. I was shocked and very uncomfortable. My space was violated and I was struggling for words and an exit strategy. In my shocked state, I guess that my voice tone rose to a new level because my husband heard it, and once he had heard, he could hear the discomfort.

He stopped in the middle of the terminal and turned to face me. <u>When he saw the man smelling my neck he didn't stop to think</u>. He just dropped his head down and ran like a linebacker at him as he lifted his war voice and screamed "Get away from my wife, now!" It was like I was watching a live reenactment of Braveheart. He ran and screamed, "That is my wife", as loud as he could. The curious man looked at me as if I could stop him and then looked at him and realized there was no stopping him. He very quickly turned and ran into a service door that would be used for staff access only as he apologized for being inappropriate.

Brian stopped as he ran up to me and asked if I was okay. I responded with robust laughter and assured him I was fine. Just about that time I heard applause and people screaming things like "Great job", "Atta boy", and "Way to go!" I think the people around were more shocked than I was.

You see, I know Brian and I knew he would show up. I had no doubt that he would protect me at all costs even if he had to look like a Viking warrior and make a scene. Needless to say, the people who observed it sitting at the airport coffee shop were amazed. They were thrilled by the thought of a husband doing his job.

Men are to protect their families at all costs. I am very aware that my life was not in danger because a man chose to smell my neck. However, knowing that Brian will protect me is a huge part of the trust we share. This trust seeps into so many areas of our relationship. I am an extremely independent and self-sufficient woman. I can handle myself and have on many occasions. This has nothing to do with me being a damsel in distress. It had everything to do with God giving Brian a job and him doing it with strength and consistency.

When I saw Brian's protection at that moment, it made it easier for me to believe that he is on my side. It isn't just about physical protection, It's bigger than that. I know that Brian will protect me physically, spiritually, and will protect my reputation. He will protect me no matter what arises and I will do the same for him. We're teammates and even if we have a disagreement, I am much more likely to see him as an ally that might be trying to help me. This is because, he always jumps in to protect me when he has an opportunity instead of treating me like a foe that he needs to fight against. I know that I can trust him to be there for me.

I have never played football but I would imagine that it is incredibly important for the quarterback to trust his teammates. If he is going be able to focus on getting the ball down the field he will need to feel comfortable with his team. If he experiences a play where they all stand still and let him get sacked, it will affect his performance. It would be a long time before he would run a play with no thought about his safety. He is already a target because he has the ball. If he knows that his team is fighting off his attackers he will be far more likely to focus on the goal and running plays with excellence. If he is worried about his back he will be distracted. Looking behind instead of focused ahead. This is a really good way to lose a game.

If you want to win in this life you need a teammate that has your back. If you feel vulnerable you are much more likely to miss your mark. If you know your teammate is good at what they do, you can just run! Run far and fast, win, and win again. If you want your marriage to win, the best thing you can do is decide what a win is and then put your jersey on.

There were many times during the early years of our marriage that I struggled with allowing Brian to protect me, especially emotionally. I was young and under the impression that if I had any relational hardships with my family it was best for me to address those with my family and for Brian to handle things with his family. For the most part, I still see this as wise if you have anything that you need to discuss with a family member or friend. Even if the person you need to have a heart-to-heart with is from your husband's family or maybe a friend or co-worker. We should go ahead and address that concern as an adult. It can be incredibly uncomfortable to be required to deal with someone's overprotective spouse that may not even understand the relationship or the details. If you live long enough you will be required to have a constructive yet confrontational conversation in life. I am a friendly person and I do not naturally like conflict, It actually makes me sick to my stomach but I absolutely love people being happy. I would prefer conflict being something other people deal with but I have found that it is inevitable at times for me to be involved.

I had a family member my entire life that would get upset often. I could always appease this person. At least for a small space of time but they would inevitably get angry with everyone in the family again and blow up. I was usually the one that everyone would send to make it better. I never settled the issue but I was really good at getting them to back off and allow life to go back to a semi-normal state. We would all walk on eggshells and give this person their way and it seemed to work out.

Well, this all seemed to come to a head when I married Brian. He would speak his mind, because he was young and outspoken. He had opinions and was encouraged to have his own mind in his family. This was not something that my family perceived as a plus but I loved it. He was honest but extremely happy for you to be honest as well. If he didn't like what I said he would tell me he disagreed but never forced me to take his opinion as my own. After, he would ask me if I wanted to go grab some food! He is quick to move on and even speedy to forgive.

I had never experienced this and I knew it wasn't going to be popular with this specific family member of mine. In fact, I would go to great lengths to never allow a serious subject to be discussed in their presence. I would wring my hands and get a stomach ache if anything ever came up that they didn't like. I begged Brian after we got married to not address off-limit topics so I wouldn't have more work to do in fixing things. He would respect my request, but he would always remind me that it was okay to disagree and very abnormal to have to bow and bend to one person every day to keep them happy.

I thought he just didn't get it. It was so normal to me that I couldn't imagine living any other way until I moved away and started living without this pressure for months on end. As I observed other families I found that they didn't do this. After about my tenth psychology class I realized that it was not normal but it was abusive!

When this became unveiled in my life I struggled. I struggled to see it for what it was and had a very hard time stopping myself from trying to be the fixer. This became easier as I stopped fixing other people's issues with this family member. When they would decide to come after me I would immediately fall back into my old ways of satisfying and trying to make it better while I walked on eggshells. Brian would get so upset because he loved me and he couldn't stand to watch! I would beg him year after year to stay out of it. He might comment here or there if this person would yell and berate me long enough but for the most part, he tried to stay out of it.

About thirteen years into our marriage nothing had changed, we were on a roller coaster that seemed to be getting worse. No matter what I tried I could not make this person happy and they continued to torment me emotionally.

I was on a trip to South Korea visiting and being trained at Dr. Paul Yongi Cho's church which at the time was one of the top two largest churches in the world. At one time his church was made up of one million members. My heart was expecting something big that week. I especially prepared for a trip to what is known as Prayer Mountain. People come from all over the world to fast and pray in this special spot and I just knew that I was going to encounter God there.

I went up to the mountain that day saying, "I will come back with a life-changing word!" I was so excited and I had never been so expectant. I had a hundred things for God to talk with me about and things I deemed important. I was waiting to hear him speak. I waited, prayed, listened sang, and prayed again. FINALLY, I heard God speak so clearly. It was so undeniably clear that I was sure it was God and to be honest I was just shocked that God wasted his time.

"Let Brian do his job," I asked, "What Lord?" He said it again, "Release Brian to do his job!". There was no question what God was talking about but I still could not believe God cared. I was stunned and a little disappointed because I wanted a "word from heaven".

When I returned to the hotel I shared my experience with Brian. He said, "Thank goodness I've been wanting to protect you but you wouldn't allow me." I had no idea he felt that strongly about it. The next time this family member came around to call me out, set me straight, yell at me until I cried, and tell me what a terrible person I was, Brian stepped in.

Then, he did it again the next time and the next. It didn't take long for this person to stop wanting to hang out. Peace came to me in a measure that I had never lived in.

Life became happier, routines changed, and my stress level went down. I stopped having physical pain from ribs popping out of place due to stress and muscle tension. I was amazed at the difference that word from God made. I thought I could handle it but God's plan was for the husband in our home to stand up. He did it with kindness, respect, and love but He did it anyway!

When they yelled, he said it anyway. When they cried, he stuck to his guns. When they talked badly about me, he didn't back up. He had exactly what the situation needed. A God-given authority to protect his wife and children. It isn't always physical, sometimes it is spiritual or emotional! Protection comes in all different shapes and sizes but it is the will of God.

I realized husbands are called by God to love their wives like they love their own bodies. To protect and provide, to Love and feed them because no one lets themselves starve or be injured if they can stop it. No one with a healthy mind would allow themselves to be harmed.

I want to encourage every woman that is reading this book to allow yourself to be protected by your husband. When life hurts, lean into the man God placed in your marriage with you. When finances are scary, please lean into your husband. When you don't have an answer to the problem that your family is in, or you're not sure which job opportunity you should take, lean in. If you aren't sure of yourself or your "new self" due to age, birthing babies, life circumstances, or even pain that has changed you, lean in. Never, never, underestimate the power of leaning into the man God called to protect you. He didn't just give him to you so you could have him in the house or eat dinner with someone. He isn't there to just be a companion.

I want to encourage every spouse to take their rightful spot. Don't let people attack or put down your wife or husband. Stand up for them. Be their strong arm. Sometimes it's easy if it is family (especially if it is your family) to leave them to fend for themselves but when they make snide comments or tease them harshly about a weakness they have, defend them as you would a friend, and don't leave them alone and searching for encouragement. Be the first one to compliment your spouse, be the first to find the one thing they cook that isn't terrible, and focus on their strengths in public. If you need to bring up something negative to them do that in private.

God gave you that man to bring protection to your heart, emotions, self-esteem, body, finances, mental health, kids, and the people you love. The biggest temptation in times of crisis is to rely only on oneself, and we do this for many reasons.

Insecurity in our relationship is a big one. Maybe you haven't even been married long enough to trust him to do his God-given job. You may not be sure that, if you turn this over to him, he will succeed and this brings anxiety, which quickly turns into insecurity and lack of confidence.

Habit is another reason for not leaning into your spouse, and old habits are hard to break. You may have had another person in your life like a dad, ex-husband, or heck maybe your current guy has failed enough times in this area, that you have sworn that no man will ever get another chance. Give yourself the freedom and approval that you need to try again.

If it has been an issue in the past then I encourage you to seek professional help and accountability. Give it a chance when it is time. Maybe even start with something small and work your way up. Whatever you do, don't blame yourself if your spouse doesn't handle it well, and do not close your heart off. God will step in and help you but a closed heart is assurance that you will never live in this blessing God called you to.

In a day and age where women chastise men if they hold the door open, I want to encourage all the men to keep it up. Don't stop, please keep up the chivalry. I believe the pendulum will swing back and we will get there. We need to know we are protected and that at a very core level, you love us enough to lay down your life, even if it simply means discomfort. We need to see you stand when we approach a table. We need to have our car doors opened. It's not because we're not strong enough to open them ourselves, it is because we need to know that we are worth it, that we are worth anything and everything.

We are not the only ones that need this. Our daughters need to see it, granddaughters, and even our friends who are divorced or single, who haven't ever seen this beautiful thing, they need to see it! They need to understand what real love from a real man looks like. It doesn't look flippant. It looks intentional and protective. It looks like he believes he has stumbled upon something precious enough to cherish.

When God gave us commands in scripture, usually, they served a face value need. I believe in the area of marriage the scripture serves to build something inside both the husband and the wife. The protection of a man builds a woman as she understands her value in his eyes; the Bible also helps women to see their value in the eyes of our Savior. Similarly, God uses this principle to build a man and to give him great purpose. When he understands that purpose and engages in it he receives an amazing level of self-esteem and self-respect which goes a long way in life. Feeling like a winner in relationships translates to winning in every area of your life.

The man protects and as he does this he understands that he is valuable to the family. He is a warrior that fights to protect God's greatest illustration of His love for His bride (the Church) on earth. The world needs to see protection in marriage because they need to understand the protection of God is available through salvation.

You see, as married couples, we are never just fighting for our marriage. We are fighting to represent, to the world, the beautiful relationship that is God and His church. He has asked us to be His illustrated message. We are the only picture they will see of His love for them. This is why the devil fights us in marriage. He fights us and desires that we fail because he doesn't want anyone to see too many beautiful representations of God's love and care for His bride. What a beautiful position we are in when we choose to be a part of God's illustrated message.

—Pastor Jessi Gibson

LOVE HANDLE:

Show your spouse your protection. Show chivalry or show gratefulness for that chivalry. Practice protection in a specific way. Protect their reputation by not speaking evil of them. Protect them spiritually through prayer. There are so many ways to follow this command. Both husbands and wives can practice protection.

Before Disney went "WOKE!!"

CHAPTER 3:

LOVE HANDLES WINNING

"For whatever is born of God overcomes
the world. And this is the victory that
has overcome the world—our faith."
I John 5:4 NKJV

"WHEN THE PHILADELPHIA EAGLES WON THE SUPERBOWL IN 2018 THEY GAVE A RING TO EVERY VALUABLE PLAYER."

"In their generous organization, even the Janitor was given a Superbowl ring. I love this fact because it reminds me of the family. If we make a champion family we all get the reward, no one that contributed is ever left in the cold. The win is greater than the winning play or any specific winning player. The win is the goal and it is the most important thing.

We help, support, run, work, practice, stay, and then, when the prizes and rewards are distributed we all receive them for playing our position well.

Sometimes we forget that we have a position in the Christian marriage. God set that up well in scripture. God's roster doesn't shift because people have decided they don't like the lineup and culture doesn't get to decide how we will play. Our family members' disapproval of the order, and our friend's disagreement with the lineup, will not change God's word. No, God is the coach and He decides who will play where. Anywhere that God places us is going to be the perfect place to hang out.

There is no second-guessing God. God knows the end from the beginning, and the same God that began a good work in you on your wedding day will be faithful to complete that work. The quicker we give in to His purpose and plan, the better off we will be. He never positions us poorly. Playing on the team is the main thing and any position on a God team is way better than no position at all! Anything outside of God's plan creates chaos and inevitably it will cost us the win."

— Pastor Brian Gibson

YOU MUST DECIDE WHAT THE WIN IS

"Most people enter into a marriage internally deciding what is fair and then we write a script for our spouse."

I was definitely guilty of this when I was newly married. Most of the time we never share the script with our spouse or our children. We just expect, that if they are good people, they will play their part. This is a losing scenario, because people do not think the same as you. Ideas and goals are different, and we must learn to communicate "the play" with our teammate (spouse). If we all know the play we are far more likely to win and if they mess up we cover them.

When trust is built every day, knowing that everyone involved wants the team to win, then we are well on our way to having winning seasons. We are one and people begin to view us as one, even in the natural world. Winning represents every family member being involved.

Every family (by family I mean the unit that is formed the minute a man and woman say I do) defines winning differently. Don't wait until you have children to build and define your family. You are a team the minute that you come into a covenant with one another. Children deserve the right of entering a family when they are born, and shouldn't be required to be the start of that creation.

You and your spouse alone decide what your personal definition of winning looks like. Your win will most likely look very different to you as individuals, but if you don't communicate and come up with your own family wins, you may find yourselves losing no matter how hard you both work. That can be a very frustrating scenario. You will most likely pull from what your childhood looked like, or possibly fight for the exact opposite. Chances are that both of you are very different from each other. This does not make creating a great marriage impossible but it does require work in order for your marriage to succeed.

One of you may end the day and feel like you lost and your spouse didn't even try, while the other works hard and feels the same way about you. **I encourage you to sit down and ask each other what a win would look like to you. You might be shocked at their answer.** It may be polar opposite to yours, or very similar. It may also be the polar opposite of what you thought they would say. You need to know what a daily win is for your family. You also need to know what a lifetime win looks like. Then and only then can you properly gauge your success.

If you don't take the time to invest in this "playbook" of sorts then you will constantly look for others to direct you. You will feel guilty and frustrated about things that people tell you are important, even if those things aren't the slightest bit important to you as a couple.

I recognized this in my own life early on in our marriage. My family had always divided up household responsibilities. Saturdays were cleaning day, then another day of the week every child was responsible for our own laundry. When I entered marriage at nineteen I was still a part of this system and living at home. I moved from my family home directly into our newlywed apartment.

Brian and I were both in college and Brian had a job after his classes ended, so I would clean and cook and do his laundry as well as my own. This seemed normal to me because he was working and I wasn't at the time. It also seemed normal to Brian because he was from a family where his mother oversaw everything domestic and did not require her children to do household chores. He had never been asked to do anything inside the home because he was raised on a farm and worked out on that farm every extra hour that he wasn't at school or football during the majority of the year.

For the first five years of our marriage this worked well and we continued to live in that system. Soon we planted a church, had a baby and I was working sixty, seventy, and even eighty hours a week sometimes! We both took the same day off at this point if we ever had time to take one and I just assumed he would help me clean that day. Because my family ran this way I assumed that Brian would jump right in and help, and he didn't!

I stayed angry about it, nagged and pressured him all the time. In my mind, he just needed a nudge (or shove maybe) to get back in the process with me and he wasn't understanding how much help I needed. He would get up and say "I'll see ya later" with his golf clubs in hand. I was exhausted and had a preconceived idea that he just assumed I would clean.

Finally, I said "I don't want to stay here and clean either. I work as many hours as you do and I'm exhausted. Why do you assume it's my responsibility to keep this place clean?" He responded by saying."Well, I don't expect you to stay and do it either. If we skip eating out once a week we can hire someone to do it for us." At this moment I realized how vital it is to communicate.

In my mind, he was being unkind by leaving me there. In his mind, I liked doing it.

My family never let someone come in and help with household chores. They made a valid and perfectly legitimate choice but it wasn't the only option for a family. Brian was different. His family had needed help running their business, farm, and help around the house and with kids in order to support his mother's ability to take care of the financial office of that business. It was perfectly normal in his experience to work long grueling hours and then come home and do family activities or rest if you found a day to do so.

Because I assumed something instead of talking about it, and creating a winning game plan for our family, I had endured years of anger and friction. I had also put my family through undue stress. Another couple may see this differently and make a different choice. They may be right and this may bring peace to their house, however, this is our call to make. As simple as this problem seems now, it was really big and relationship breaking until I understood that we didn't have the same winning game plan in mind.

Never assume that you know what the win is without a real conversation. People love to give opinions but they should never get a first or second voice in your decision making. The first position belongs to The Bible and the second belongs to you and your spouse. When you have these two in order, then you don't have to be shaken by the opinions of others or moved by what other families look like on social media.

If your mother-in-law lets you know she disapproves of you but you are sure that you have an agreement with your spouse, then you can smile and nod at family dinners instead of crying or being angry when you leave. Peace is rooted in a whole lot of communication.

We are created by God to love our spouse and we can learn what is important to us and do it. God never called me to be a helpmate to Sally's husband across the street. It doesn't matter what he thinks about my job, and Brian doesn't have to impress or keep Sally happy. However, knowing what your winning game plan looks like is your responsibility, and not pressing in to figure it out can lead to a lot of frustration and relational damage. So, don't put it off, start today.

When Brian and I first got married we were very young. We had a total of two premarital classes under our belt (which honestly may have made us one of the most informed newlyweds ever). We were in love and even friends that liked each other. This did not help when we had to decide what Television program we would watch on our one twenty-inch box TV. We only had one screen to watch and we had a major problem. The football game was on! Oh yeah and a chick flick! This may seem like a silly problem but for a man raised in a house with all brothers and a woman raised in a household with all sisters, it was major.

Neither one of us had ever considered for one second that there was a choice to be made. We both knew exactly which program should be chosen and it never crossed our minds that anyone in the world would pick the opposite program. Needless to say, it ended in much frustration and shock. I don't even remember how we settled it but I am pretty sure we did a lot of channel changing during commercials and tried not to give each other dirty looks.

This wasn't going to destroy us or decide the direction of our life but it is a small glimpse inside of how different we were, and how opposite our family wins were. We had a lot of work to do!

We just started spelling it out to each other. One piece at a time, we made decisions about what our win would look like.

—Pastor Jessi Gibson

PEACE IS A WIN!

Our family has decided that peace at all costs is a huge part of our win.

> "For where envying and strife is, there
> is confusion and every evil work."
> James 3:16

"Strife is the number one thing we will not tolerate in our home."

If we are being difficult and causing trouble with each other we repent as quickly as possible. If we have a guest that brings strife into our house we invite them to leave and return when they want to live in peace. We don't allow extended family to come into our house and stir up fights. If our kids fuss we stop the conversation and remind them that they are inviting every evil thing into our house.

I illustrate it often by pretending to throw our front door open and saying "Welcome evil stuff, come on in and have your way with our family!" Dramatic? Yes! But it gets the point across and rallies my kids to participate in peace. Peace is always worth urgent repentance!

Being a peacemaker and being a peacekeeper are two different things.

Peacekeepers just say whatever the person wants to hear to stop fighting. They allow anything to continue so there will not be friction. They even allow people and/or themselves to be abused for fear that if they stand up to the abuser they may have an uncomfortable encounter. As believers, we are not called to be peacekeepers at any cost. This is a lie that many families have operated under.

No, Christianity is not a ticket for abusers to have their way with everyone in their family and not be confronted. True forgiveness comes in response to repentance. Many people will disagree. Living in goodwill toward others is important for our hearts, however, the popular forgiveness doctrine that has been around for decades puts victims in harm's way. Even God forgives people of their trespasses following genuine repentance. Forgiveness is not ignoring a problem and allowing everyone to be hurt at the hands of the difficult person, forgiveness does not always include reintroduction to the family. It doesn't give free rein to the offender to offend again, and it definitely doesn't put children in harm's way for the sake of the comfort of the abuser. True love protects the defenseless and holds accountable those who try to trespass against them.

PEACEKEEPING AND PEACEMAKING ARE USUALLY VERY DIFFERENT.

Peacemakers do whatever is necessary and even have the difficult conversations required to achieve long-term peace for everyone involved. I have been married long enough to know that there are times that everyone cannot have their own way. It is in these moments that we compromise and work to come together, but long-term peace is definitely never achieved by the same person getting their way every day or even avoiding a conversation altogether.

There are times that this process is difficult and it may even require a third party being brought in to mediate. Wisdom will be needed and if it doesn't lie within us for this particular subject we may need to seek it out. Never be embarrassed to seek wisdom, you must get it no matter what you need to do to find it.

> "Do not forsake her, and she will preserve you; Love her, and she will keep you. Wisdom is the principal thing;Therefore get wisdom.And in all your getting, get understanding."
> Proverbs 4:6-7 (NKJV)

LET YOUR REPENTANCE BE AS LOUD AS YOUR OFFENSE.

This does two things:

- It brings dignity back to the person you hurt or possibly even humiliated.

- It is a natural deterrent to aggressively offending your loved one.

If you are able to yell at your spouse or publicly ridicule them, only then to come with a very weak apology that includes a lot of "but's" and very little repentance (turning the opposite direction), then you are more likely to offend again. Something about your repentance not being in a whisper after you publicly hurt someone is healing for this individual and brings restraint in your next encounter.

Never whisper your repentance. Too many times we scream in public and apologize in private. If we want real relationships that flourish we will demand more of ourselves than this.

—Pastor Jessi Gibson

A GREAT REPUTATION IS A WIN

```
"And above all things have fervent love
for one another, for "love will cover a
multitude of sins.""
I Peter 4:8
```

"We believe that love covers
a multitude of sins."

It is never our goal to expose each other's weaknesses or mistakes, but instead to cover them.

In the midst of the garden after the first sin was committed by Adam and Eve, I am certain that God was more than disappointed, He was heartbroken. He didn't scream and yell. He didn't create extra humans to call and bad mouth them. God in His great love and desire for relationship instead made garments and covered their shame. Wow! God, in all His holiness and righteousness, did not choose to expose them and embarrass them. He chose to cover and love them.

We are called to protect our spouse's reputation. Make each other look good if you will. In fact, I believe it is the heart of God for us to make each other look even better than we might actually be that day. The Bible tells us that two are better than one. This is because if one has a weak moment, or God forbid, a weak year, we can pick up their slack. If our spouse has off days it is our moment to step up and shine.

We can be controlled in our temper and kind to our neighbors. People in our community then see our spouse as kind. Our reputations matter. We control some of that in our communities. We affect how people see our family. Every individual is responsible for their own actions but we definitely help.

Think of a president. We see him and his political decisions but they keep the wife of that President very close by at all times because she is a representation of the President. What kind of person has he chosen to be closest to? Is he a good decision maker? Is he a great leader? Does she look like an individual who has been emotionally nurtured? Does he like intelligent people around or does he just want to crush everyone under his "leadership"? What matters to her? The more intelligent and happy she appears, the better people feel about that leader.

Wives are like a sneak peek into who a man is in private. Men are a representation in the city gates of the family. I like to think of the husband as a well-designed label on a great product, and the family as a whole as that "great product".

He represents who they are and what they are made of but you never get to enjoy it fully unless you get an opportunity to know the family.

We decided years ago that we can bless people that the other spouse missed in their distraction. We can Cover each other's failures, speak to people that the other forgot, sneek money under pillows early in the morning because the other one accidentally fell asleep early. We can even sign the other spouse's name to gifts they never even realized needed to be purchased. We can do all this and never expose each other's weaknesses.

I benefit from Brian's children adoring him and the community we live in thinking well of him. It is good for our entire family if people feel loved by him. We all benefit from having great relationships in our community and that cannot hurt us. The only harm is in us having no good relationships because I needed credit more than I needed a win.

"Teamwork makes the dream work." Maybe that saying is a little cheesy but it is oh so true."Team Gibson" winning is more important than me carrying the ball and being interviewed after the game. Sometimes in marriage and family, we get hyper-focused on everyone doing their part that day. There is one problem with this idea. There are many days in marriage that just aren't fairly distributed. There are days that I carry eighty percent and Brian carries twenty percent, but the next day he will be required to carry one hundred percent because of sickness or other circumstances that arise.

We cannot let this make us bitter. If we buy into the fifty/fifty concept we will be disappointed. Instead, we can come into marriage with a one hundred percent concept. Every day I'm showing up in this relationship hoping to serve, give, and participate one hundred percent.

We have a saying in our home that we repeat regularly to remind ourselves, "It's not fair, it's family." This statement is not meant to let any individual person off the hook but instead to prepare everyone for their part in the day. If it doesn't go our way, but our family wins, we still consider it a win. If we have to give more than expected that day but "Team Gibson" ends the day with a win, then we have personally won. No team player ever goes to the victory party with a list of things they had to do during the game that were unfair. No, they just cheer and eat the cake because winning is more important than anything.

– *Pastor Jessi Gibson*

PRODUCTIVITY IS A WIN

"Work ethic has always been a huge part of our family culture."

"For even while we were with you, we used to give you this order: if anyone is not willing to work, then he is not to eat, either." II Thessalonians 3:10 AMP

Even at dinner, it is known that if a "Gibson" isn't willing to help with setting the table or cleaning they will not be partaking in the food. We get up and we produce every day, we love and celebrate a job well done.

We are doing everything we can to educate and make our children readers. This gives them a hand up in being productive members of society. We don't settle, we strive for excellence in every area. When human beings produce something in work, we understand winning, and the more we win, the more comfortable we are with winners. We want our family to feel out of place in non-productive environments. Our Pastor always says "How you do anything, is how you do everything!" So, we do things well. Hopefully, we will leave a legacy of the joy of hard work for our grandchildren.

—Pastor Jessi Gibson

PURITY IS A WIN

"At all costs, we should protect our homes."

Purity before God and in our marriage are vital to a healthy family. People talk about keeping themselves pure before marriage. We do this through sexual abstinence and guarding what comes in front of our eyes and into our ears. People sometimes find this difficult in our current culture but there are so many blessings attached to this way of living.

> "But women will be saved through childbearing, assuming they continue to live in faith, love, holiness, and modesty". 1 Timothy 2:15-3:7 NLT

God never asks for something unnecessary. He never steals from us. It is not in God's nature to steal, he only adds life to us through our obedience and accountability to His word. People rarely consider the purity that will be required of them after marriage. Lust is no respecter of persons, and wedding bands don't ward off temptation. Purity is equally needed before and after a wedding. True purity is obedience to God in every season, not just sexual abstinence before the covenant of marriage.

It is just as pure to be sexually active in marriage as it is sexually abstinent outside of marriage!

That being said, it is vital that we understand the parameters given and abide by them before and after marriage. It is also really big that we guard our hearts and if we have children we are needed to help protect their hearts.

-Pastor Jessi Gibson

FUN IS A WIN

"A merry heart does good, like medicine: but a broken spirit dries the bones." Proverbs 17:22 NKJV

"WE WANT TO WORK HARD AND THEN PLAY JUST AS HARD."

The sabbath is not a bondage but a gift to Christians given by God to rest the entire being. Part of the win for our family is laughter and joy being a part of every day. We celebrate the wins and the milestones. The birthdays and the anniversaries. The seasons and holidays are a part of our tradition of celebration, and we use them to teach our kids about God's kindness. People tend to take God out of holidays, or make them so "God somber" that kids have no fun. Our goal is to show our kids the kindness of God in these seasons.

Jessi and I decided years ago that we are going to make life so fun at our house that when our kids get to decide where they will spend their time, they just want to run home. The happiest place on the planet isn't Disney; it is the "Gibson house!"

Joy and fun are a part of our win and we refuse to live without laughter. Mourning and sadness steal their spots in life with no warning. They become unwelcome house guests at times, so, we have decided to invite joy in as a permanent family member.

We dance as often as we have an opportunity. We laugh about everything, even if it means we have to laugh at ourselves. We celebrate everything we can find to celebrate.

-Pastor Brian Gibson

LOVE HANDLE:

Write down your family "WIN" on a piece of paper and then let the other one read it. Discuss what you share in common, and what it will look like for you both to be settled in your pursuit of success. Be sure to include roles in the home, with children, employment, and pursuit of one another. Please remember that this will need a lot of development and attention. This is not a one-hour or one-day thing. It will take time and discovery.

Think about celebrations. When was the last time you celebrated something as a family? Do you always focus on sickness, disease, lack of money, hardship? Have you danced lately? Yes, you! The one who doesn't dance very well. Don't hesitate. God loves to hear you laugh, and celebration is a win. Make a plan to celebrate something in your family today. On a whim, just turn on some music while you make dinner or drive to an obligation. Now, open your mouth and sing the words, even if you get the lyrics wrong! You've got this.

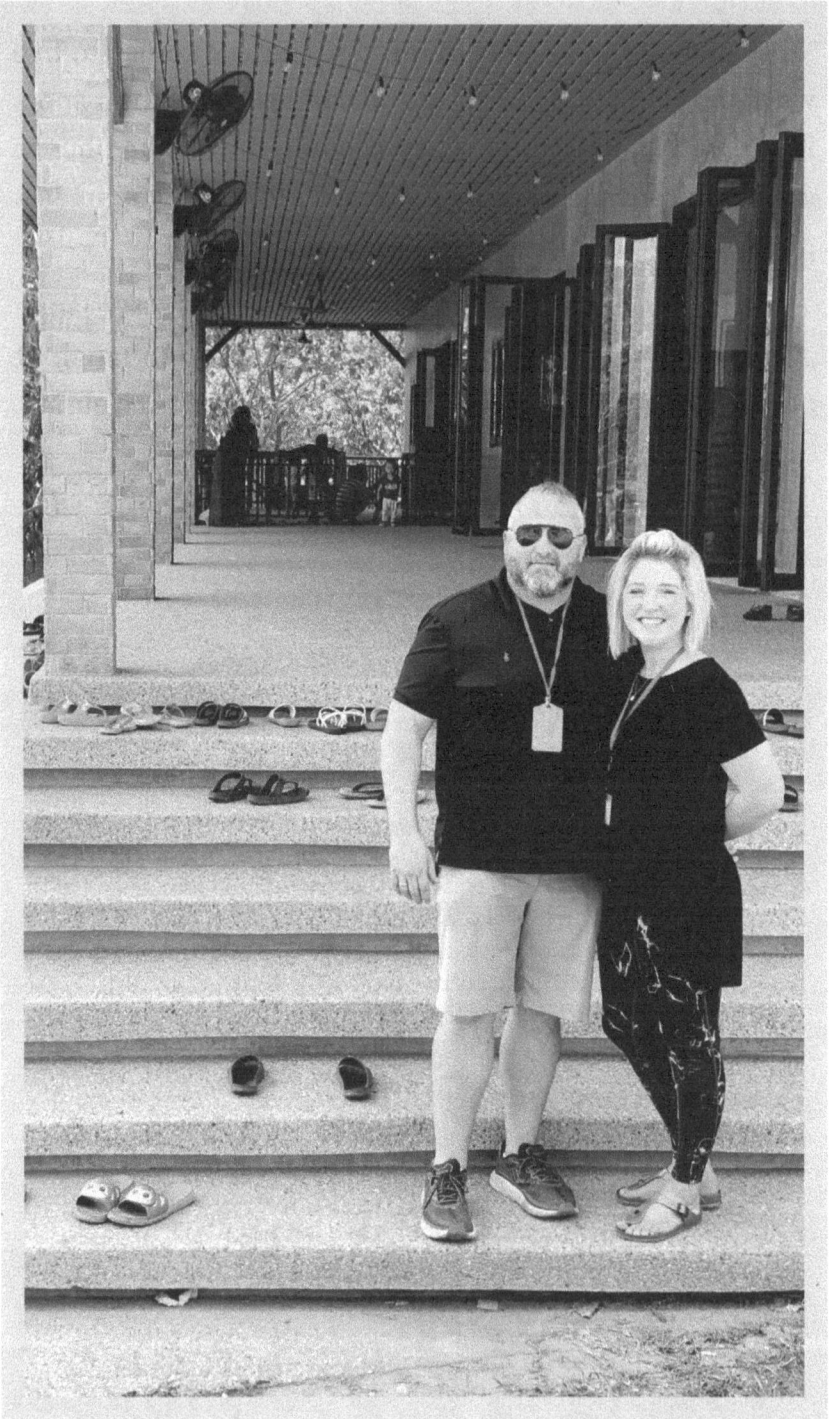

CHAPTER 4:

LOVE HANDLES FEAR

God gives us the perfect way to let love deal with our fear.

> "There is no fear in love; but perfect love casts out fear, because fear involves torment. But he who fears has not been made perfect in love." I John 4:18 NKJV

"The fact is that Jesus is love. He doesn't just act in love or show love."

He doesn't even just embody love. He IS love. It flows from him and is given from him. The source of all love is Jesus.

I believe with all my heart that this is one of the main reasons that God tells us in 2 Corinthians 6:14 ESV not to "be unequally yoked with unbelievers. For what partnership has righteousness with lawlessness? Or what fellowship has light with darkness." Most people think that God is instructing us not to be partnered together in dating, marriage, business, or any other venture that puts two people in a position of equal work or gain.

Some believe that God is trying to cut their options, or steal their fun. I have even had people ask if God is trying to remove anyone remotely handsome and interesting from the playing field. As funny as that sounds, people start to believe that God has it out for them because he doesn't allow people who know the light and love of God to partner with people who do not. Little do they know that God is trying to protect them.

When this issue is addressed as it pertains to marriage many people get frustrated. We as humans are trying to find the perfect person for us. All the while, God is giving us guard rails that will ensure that we win in life. At the end of the day, we will be in covenant with them and this is a room with no exits, this is forever. This covenant is to be until death. Of all the partnerships in the world, this one is the most Holy. The Bible actually says that we become one. That should give us pause as we begin to think about who we will unite our lives with.

Marriage is one of the biggest choices of your life. I know, I know, you want me to take the pressure out of what I'm saying because it makes you nervous. You are begging God to show you the perfect "one". Well, news flash, you can't find the perfect one because they don't exist. However, God does give us guidance and wisdom and this is one of the top pieces of the marriage puzzle.

Is the person you are thinking of dating, dreaming of marrying, or engaged to detrimental to the Person that you are already in covenant with? Are they a believer in Jesus as the crucified and risen Son of God? Do they believe that He came once to die, and will return again as a lion to take His Church and judge the nations. Sounds serious? That is because it is.

One of the best pictures God gives us is being yoked to our spouse. If we need to move forward and we are yoked like two oxen at the neck, we will need to have a unified approach. If you try to go forward and your teammate sits down, you are going to be frustrated and inevitably never get as far as you could have. Even in your obedience, you would be dragging dead weight.

If you both know and obey the same God then you are more likely to move together. If God says stop, you both stop. If he says move, you both move. If he tells you to give and you share that with a spouse that is in sync with God, they are more likely to agree to obey, even if they don't hear it themselves, because they will learn to trust that God is speaking.

A lot of people get frustrated because they date and marry anyone they want. They never ask God if He agrees. They never find out if that person actually reads the Bible, loves Jesus, and has a church or a Pastor (this is important because it shows that they are submitted spiritually to leadership, and you cannot lead if you cannot follow). Then they want God to somehow make them an easier person to be yoked up to. They want to follow God but they are stuck in the mud with a partner that refuses to move. Their life isn't what they want it to be. This can be very frustrating, and if we are honest, a little scary.

I believe this is one of the reasons that God asked us not to be unequally yoked with anyone that doesn't possess LOVE. I mean the actual embodiment of love, and His name is Jesus. This relationship with Jesus inside your covenant casts out fear. Why? Because you understand at a very core level that this person hears from and knows the same God that is directing you.

This fact may not seem that important at the beginning of a relationship when you are going to dinner, dancing on the weekends, and playing putt-putt to pass the time. It may seem trivial because you are not yoked at the neck trying to pull the weight of life together. But please just imagine with me a day when you are linked to this partner.

Imagine a day when you are starting a family, a business, trying to pay bills, discipline toddlers, walk through a death in the family, laid off from a great job, doing the best job you know to do in raising teenagers, have to make decisions about a move, God forbid lose a child or fight a terminal illness.

Who do you trust to hear God's voice? Who do you trust with your life? Who do you want beside you to hold your hand and mourn with you, but then stop you and put a demand on your faith? Tell you that it is time to fight and not to give up? These days come and life has a way of leaving you lost in fear or lifted in faith based on who you surround yourself with. Do they know God's voice? Can they hear it clearly? Is this person the kind of person that obeys quickly and is secure in their ability to hear God's leading? Do you trust them? Do they have perfect love flowing in their life? Then and only then will fear disappear.

I will never forget the night that I found myself more grateful than ever that I had listened to God's instruction for partnering together with a man who knows Jesus. I had lost a baby in miscarriage a few months before becoming pregnant with our second child. The pain of miscarriage was a lot for this young mother. People already knew and I was 10 weeks along when the heartbeat stopped. I was so sad, embarrassed (I have no idea why this was an emotion I experienced deeply), and all together disappointed.

Something about miscarriage made me feel like I had somehow let my child down. I am intelligent enough to understand that I didn't do anything to cause this but my heart was aching and my brain was not doing the thinking. I was completely emotional.

It took two months before I was pregnant again. I was very vigilant, excited, happy, and yet still a little gun shy. After all, the last pregnancy seemed perfect until it wasn't. Unlike the other pregnancy, this baby continued to grow past 10 weeks and my heart became stronger with every passing week. I am a faith girl so I just kept speaking God's word over my baby every day, and I even had a man of God tell me that I would "conceive quickly and bear a son"! This was between the miscarriage and the current pregnancy so I held onto this word from God and claimed it every time fear tried to creep in.

At twenty-six weeks gestation I felt something funny one night as I laid on the couch watching television. Yep, I knew that feeling, I was having contractions. NO! I could not have a baby at twenty-six weeks, that's too risky and the baby isn't ready was all I could think. However, the contractions continued until I was having one every five minutes. I told my husband something was wrong and he rushed me to the hospital.

People were rushing around and Brian was pacing. My doctor soon made an appearance and explained the risks attached to a baby being born this early and what they were going to do to stop my labor. He told us about the side effects of those drugs and said it was important for me to relax. Yeah, that's right, relax. All I could think was "No way am I losing this little boy!" I will fight in the spirit and keep him.

I began to remind God of his word. According to the Bible, I am "a fruitful vine that does not cast her fruit before her time", "my leaf will not wither," and "whatever I put my hand to it prospers". I was using the sword of the spirit (the word of God) to fight this battle. Then I remembered the word I received over this child so I began to remind myself and the devil that God said: "I would conceive quickly and

BARE a son." I stood on that word as I believed that his life would not be lost.

I fought for hours just praying and believing. It was about this time that they came in to give me some medicine to hopefully make me sleep. I didn't like that idea because I wanted to stay awake and fight (I am a fighter by nature). The thought crossed my mind "If I go to sleep no one will fight." I was wrong, because the Bible promises that God fights while we sleep. At this point, I had a major revelation. I chose a husband ten years before this moment, that knows Jesus. He hears his voice and he obeys it, knows the Bible, is faith fit for this battle and it is vital that my focus be on rest. So, I turned to him and said," Brian, I have to rest and you have to fight. Whatever you do, don't leave and don't stop fighting in the spirit. This little boy will come strong and right on time." He said, "I've got this."

Those three words changed my life. I realized in a very different way because of the situation that God had not taken away options when I was looking for a mate. Instead, he had given me a partner to fight with me for the good of our family. He was my hero, my gift from God, and I can't fathom what I would have done if I didn't trust him. I was so grateful. They were able over the next twenty-two hours to get my labor under control and after seven and a half weeks of bed rest and one week in the hospital because well... I am terrible at bed rest. Our son, Justice Samuel was born five weeks early but perfect. I learned a lot about prayer and trusting God and Brian. He had almost No health issues and not one day in the NICU! Praise Jesus for His mercy. He has been our healthiest child and our Pediatrician says that he is the healthiest kid in his practice.

Questioning God and his promises just brings frustration. Building our lives around those promises brings joy.

You see it is true that perfect love casts fear out. Jesus is the perfect love and if we allow Him to be the rock of our marriage then we ensure that fear has no place and peace can guide us.

CHAPTER 5:

LOVE HANDLES LIES

"You are of your father the devil, and the desires of your father you want to do. He was a murderer from the beginning, and does not stand in the truth, because there is no truth in him. When he speaks a lie, he speaks from his own resources, for he is a liar and the father of it."
John 8:44 NKJV

"TELL A LIE ONCE AND YOU MIGHT GET AWAY WITH IT."

Tell a lie twice and you might get caught. Tell a lie three times and it might just become the truth.

Lies destroy marriages! I'm not talking about the kind of lies that you're thinking about, I'm not talking about the lies you tell, I'm talking about the lies you believe.

The scripture calls the devil "the Father of Lies!"

Telling the truth does not come easy for the Devil because there is absolutely no truth in him. His nature is to simply spread falsehood. He has worked double-time to distort the truth about marriage around the world. If you were to sit down and interview him and ask him some questions it would go something like this:

> You: Are you the fallen angel that is commonly called the Devil?
>
> The Devil: No (calmly).
>
> You: I'm positive that you are the devil!?
>
> The Devil: Well, that's not entirely true.
>
> You: Are you not also commonly referred to as Lucifer?
>
> The Devil: I prefer Lou....
>
> You: Are you the entity that has been deceiving, distorting, and destroying the truth on the planet earth?
>
> The Devil: No, let's just say I help people find their own truth.

As you noticed in our interview it was extremely difficult for the devil to answer any question in a direct manner. He either directly lies or twists the truth. He has been doing this since the beginning of human history. It was the devil that tempted the first married couple to do what? To believe a lie! If we believe the lies of the enemy we will produce the fruit of that lie. Our thoughts shape our results.

I want to take a look at some commonly believed lies that have been seeded into our culture. If we can break the back of these lies we can stop their power to destroy marriages in our families and churches.

LIE NUMBER 1. MARRIAGE IS JUST TOO HARD

The whole world wants you to believe that it is darn near impossible to make a marriage work. I think the devil has sown that seed into the DNA of America. People who have failed at marriage want to make everyone believe that it is impossible to stay married. Let me make this clear - I am for people, whether they have failed or succeeded! However, I am not for people projecting their failures on others.

It's human nature to project failure on someone else. It makes you feel better about your own shortcomings when you make a task sound impossible. Parents that couldn't make things happen for one reason or another tell their children not to get their hopes up. Don't let this happen to you! Don't let anyone else fog you with their failure. Their death is not your burial.

You hear people make statements that echo this lie all the time about how impossible marriage is:

- "The old ball and chain"
- "Have all the fun you can before the "I do!""
- "You are signing your life away."
- "Why would you get married so early on? You're only sixty-two!"

Marriage is not too hard! Living the relationship roller coaster that the world is selling is hard. The world tells us to throw off the traditional restraints of marriage and do whatever feels good and right at the time because marriage is just so hard. The Bible says something very different about the situation.

> "Good understanding gains favor, But the way of the unfaithful is hard."
> Proverbs 13:15 NKJV

The scripture states that the unfaithful life is the hard life! The relational life not lived out within God's parameters is the one that brings pain and remorse again and again. Don't buy into the "married life is tough" bit! I've watched the people that push away marriage and family for years for career and freedom. They aren't more fulfilled, they are more empty, broken, and lonely. Americans have been told to push back the responsibility of family. Follow your dreams and extend your adolescence because you deserve it! Sleep around with everyone and express yourself sexually because it's the twenty-first century. If you sift to the bottom of that lifestyle you will find deep confusion and pain!

BEING THE 38 YEAR OLD PERSON AT THE CLUB LOOKING TO SCORE DOES NOT LOOK GOOD ON ANYONE!

This is a toxic mindset on marriage. Marriage was not created to be a burden, it was created to be a blessing. The way we are programmed to view marriage like a cosmic killjoy sets us up for disaster. As a man thinks in his heart so is he. If you believe that marriage is a burden you will begin to produce that in your life. If you believe that marriage is a blessing you will produce that in your life! Believe the truth - that marriage is a blessing. That marriage is the plan of God and that marriage is God's answer to a lonely, bland life. You will begin to see marriage through God's eyes and not the fallen world-systems view.

LIE NUMBER 2: 50% OF MARRIAGES END IN DIVORCE

THE STATS SHOW THAT YOU CAN'T TRUST THE STATS!

"There are three kinds of lies: lies, damn lies, and statistics."

- Prime Minister Benjamin Disraeli

British statesman and Conservative politician who twice served as Prime Minister of the United Kingdom.

This is especially true when it comes to the stats about marriage. The one stat that it seems that everyone has heard is that fifty percent of all marriages end in divorce. This stat is little more than a myth. It seems hard to find conclusive evidence on the genesis of this falsehood. Psychology Today put the stats at closer to one out of four ending in divorce.

This false statistic is setting the stage for a bad self-fulfilling prophecy for many people. It makes for thinking like this:

Yikes! If only fifty percent of couples make it in marriage then why should I keep fighting for mine? My wife and I aren't relationally more gifted than fifty percent of all Americans! I mean come on, it's a coin flip as to whether or not we will ever stay married. It's probably going to end with a split of assets and visitation rights to the kids. I'm just like the majority of people. Why in the world should I keep trying?!

Bad information leads to bad decisions! In a perfect world, we could trust the stats that we hear on such an important topic as marriage and divorce. We are talking about people's families, their children, and their futures. We aren't living in a perfect world. We are offered plenty of things to grab hold of, sometimes we are holding on to a lie.

People have skewed opinions, biases, and sometimes are just downright deceptive and evil in research. So how do statistics get around that are just wrong - someone repeats them!

Bad research can start in a variety of ways. Researchers can use small sample sets that are insignificant to draw a real conclusion. They can single out a group of people with selective bias (like asking cats their opinions about dogs!).

They can look the other way at information that doesn't back up their own personal conclusions. They can also word their surveys in such a way as to steer the participant's answers. I've heard it said that the only people who can keep their jobs and be wrong a hundred percent of the time are weathermen and statisticians.

The cards are not stacked against you. You can make it in marriage! I promise if you and your spouse will get the right information and begin to work on your relationship God will get involved in the center of your marriage.

—Pastor Brian Gibson

LIE NUMBER 3: BECAUSE MAMA LOVES ME I CAN TAKE HER MARRIAGE ADVICE.

Be Careful Who You Take Marriage Advice From!

"Where there is no counsel, the people fall; But in the multitude of counselors there is safety." Proverbs 11:14 NKJV

"I HAD A GREAT GRANDPA. AS A MATTER OF FACT, HE WAS MY FAVORITE GRANDPARENT. MY BROTHERS AND I FAVORED HIM GREATLY."

We look like him, he's a handsome devil if I do say so myself! He is always smiling and up for a good time. In life, he was probably up for a good time a little too much. We even called the race track near his home his office because he loved the horses and the ladies.

One day, my Grandpa started to offer me marriage advice. I would gladly receive advice from him about buying farms, cattle, row cropping, car trades and a variety of other business deals, but not marriage. Being raised in the Great Depression he didn't have the chance to receive much of an education as a child. His father died when he was a little boy, so he received most of his education in the school of hard knocks. Still, despite that disadvantage, he made enough money to retire early in life. He told me that he understood that he had to learn numbers. I would gladly take advice from him about business but the one area I would not receive advice about from him would be MARRIAGE!!!!!

"But Brian," you might ask, "don't you think your Grandpa loved you?" I think he absolutely loved me and wanted the best for my life, but he has been married as many times as your average Hollywood personality. He made a great boyfriend but a terrible husband.

I looked at him and said, "Grandpa, I love you. I will take advice from you about a variety of topics but why in the world would I listen to you about a woman?" He laughed out loud, until he couldn't even breathe, and told me that I was right! Just because you love someone and esteem them doesn't mean they have the answers to every problem in your life. If you need legal advice, get an attorney. If you need financial advice, find a trusted financial advisor. If you need spiritual advice, find a devout, Christian leader. If you need marital advice, find someone with a great marriage. Real counsel is not someone who necessarily loves you, but someone with a specific base of knowledge!

> "He who walks with wise men will be wise, But the companion of fools will be destroyed."
> Proverbs 13:20 NKJV

Jessi and I have sought out people like this for two decades. We look for people with strong integrity and a strong marriage to help us shape our own family life. I'm thankful for the couples who have gone before us to beat down a path that have helped show us the way in marriage. I have watched them Pastor, raise children, and foster a relationship that stood strong for decades. When I see strength like that, I want to listen to what they have to say about the topic.

Most people take advice from whoever they have around them in life. It's easier for them to talk to the people they already know than it is to seek out a mentor with real knowledge. It's easier to look for the person with the latest post on social media than to study the scriptures. But taking the easiest path to advice might prove to shape the hardest life.

Bad advice is around in abundance. Some of the people that are giving you bad advice might really love you, but that doesn't negate the fact that they are steering you in the wrong direction. It's just that they don't know any better. I want to encourage you to find someone who can help show you the way. The value of real coaching is priceless. The very fact that you picked up this book shows that you are looking for real change in your marriage. God will honor that step.

—Pastor Brian Gibson

LIE NUMBER 4:
I JUST DON'T FEEL THE LOVE ANYMORE!

"MANY PEOPLE HAVE ACCEPTED A PHILOSOPHY ON RELATIONSHIPS BASED ON THE IDEA OF FALLING IN LOVE!"

In this version of love and marriage it goes something like this: a young man is walking down the street on a bright and sunny day when suddenly, BAM, Cupid brings his fat, little, baby bottom along and shoots him with an arrow right in the heart! The man looks up, and behold, his eyes fall upon the most beautiful woman that he has ever seen. She looks up from her purse on the busiest day of her life and the second arrow is let go by Cupid. BOOM - It strikes her right in the heart. The two lock eyes and they are suddenly hit with a torrent of emotion, passion, and desire. They have fallen in love!

Now, there is nothing wrong with a good romance movie. There's something very human about wanting relationships to work out in the end. We also want to feel something in life. I don't think we should base our life on our feelings, nor do I believe that we should be emotionless robots. Hollywood's version of romance has skewed the American idea of love. If love is something that we fall into, it is also something that we fall out of, but this is a lie that will destroy your marriage. Cupid isn't shooting any arrows and thankfully he isn't pulling them out of our hearts either!

Romantic feelings are built and grow as they are fed. You can build your romantic life. If you have lost that loving feeling, I have good news for you today! You can get it back. People often start with an attraction toward one another. Then, they feed that attraction with positive relational deposits and it grows into something stronger. Often, after they say, "I do," they begin to lower the relational deposits. Sometimes they move into something more negative. They actually start making withdrawals from the relationship in a negative sense. Their relational patterns start trending downward, and as they do, so does that loving feeling. They didn't fall out of love. They created a negative pattern in their relationship.

If they will both decide to change the patterns in their relationship then they can change the feelings that they have for one another. You don't fall into love, you pattern yourself into love and you also pattern yourself out of love. You can change your feelings and emotions for one another. You can feed that feeling. Instead of being the person that falls in and out of love, you can build a real, covenant love that lasts a lifetime.

LIE NUMBER 5: I CAN'T CHANGE!

The devil loves to lie to people about their ability to change. I have lost track of how many people I've heard say, "You don't understand, this is just the way that I am." Nothing could be further from the truth! **We are what we are because of the environment we have lived in, the things that we have believed, and the decisions that we have made.** If the person that we have become is sabotaging the most important relationship in our life, we need to allow the Holy Spirit to change that person. You can change!

> "And do not be conformed to this world, but be transformed by the renewing of your mind, that you may prove what is that good and acceptable and perfect will of God." Romans 12:2 NKJV

God already wants to change us for the better. His desire is that we might become more Christ-like every day. The scripture tells us that we are to not live life the way the world lives because the world believes that it is trapped in its own patterns. We believe that we can be transformed. You can be transformed into an incredible spouse, become a super husband or a super wife! The key is simply renewing your mind. To get the results that God wants you to have in your marriage, you must begin to train your brain to think the thoughts of God. Right now, as you read this book, your mind is being renewed by the Word of God. Your character is being changed and your marriage is being transformed.

When Jessi and I first married I knew very little about the female species. I was raised in a house with three brothers and to say that the culture of our home was male would be the understatement of the year. Every one of us played football, wrestled, and had been in many fistfights. We watched sports and movies about Cowboys and mobsters. To top it all off there was a stockyard in our backyard. We were literally raised in a barn. Jessi came from a home that was exactly the opposite. In her home, there were three daughters. They did things that I had never heard of, they had a television that played networks like Lifetime. They liked to go to the mall, cuddle on the couch, do their nails, and sing together. They did things like wearing matching pajamas on Christmas Eve and I didn't even know what pajamas were!

We were in for a culture shock. I'll share a crazy story that illustrates it perfectly. It was our first Christmas Eve together. Jessi and I were living in Tulsa, Oklahoma, and we went back to her parent's home in Amarillo, Texas. The whole family was gathered in the house and Jessi's mom brought out a gift for each of us on Christmas Eve. We started to open them up and from the youngest to the oldest we all had a pair of pajamas. I said thanks to Jessi's parents. Then her mother looked at me and said, "Try them on." I told her I was fine and really didn't want to put them on. She persisted, so I asked why? She then informed me that every year her entire family put on matching pajamas and took a picture of themselves in front of the Christmas tree.

Now keep in mind that this was before social media. We had a very different grid about pictures of ourselves. To me, this seemed like the girliest, most feminine thing in the world to be a part of, so I refused the pajamas and world war three ensued. I opened up a war with Jessi's mom and the entire tribe, but I didn't care, I wasn't taking the picture.

It's funny when I look back at that night decades later. I'm pretty sure I took a photo this past Christmas in matching pajamas that said "Papa Bear" on my chest. I've learned to live in a world that isn't strictly male. I have two daughters and one son. We still watch the games and still do manly stuff. I golf, hunt, and watch the same mobster movies. I also attend tea parties for my daughter, ballet classes, recitals, and the American Girl store.

Jessi has learned to function in a world that is different as well. We have both embraced and even love change if it's for the good of our family. We have found ways to renew our minds for the good of the marriage. I don't want to stay the same year after year, I want positive change.

REFUSE THE LIES

Let's agree that we will no longer believe the lies that hold us back from becoming the greatest spouses in the world. If you have held onto one of these lies it is time to break its power over your life once and for all. You need to identify the lies that you believe are hurting your marriage. Once you identify them you need to talk about them with your spouse. It's a great way to hold each other accountable for stinking thinking.

Lies that we have believed don't go away all at once. You make a decision to change the way you think and then the work begins. The lies that we have believed will try to come back again and again. We have to learn to keep attacking the lies with the truth of the Word of God. Then and only then can we silence the lying voice forever. Jesus showed us the perfect way to silence the voice of the enemy.

"Then Jesus was led up by the Spirit into the wilderness to be tempted by the devil. And when He had fasted forty days and forty nights, afterward He was hungry.

Now when the tempter came to Him, he said, "If You are the Son of God, command that these stones become bread." But He answered and said, "It is written, 'Man shall not live by bread alone, but by every word that proceeds from the mouth of God.' " Then the devil took Him up into the holy city, set Him on the pinnacle of the temple, and said to Him, "If You are the Son of God, throw Yourself down. For it is written: 'He shall give His angels charge over you,' and, 'In their hands they shall bear you up, Lest you dash your foot against a stone.' " Jesus said to him, "It is written again, 'You shall not tempt the LORD your God.' " Again, the devil took Him up on an exceedingly high mountain, and showed Him all the kingdoms of the world and their glory. And he said to Him, "All these things I will give You if You will fall down and worship me." Then Jesus said to him, "Away with you, Satan! For it is written, 'You shall worship the LORD your God, and Him only you shall serve.' " Then the devil left Him, and behold, angels came and ministered to Him." Matthew 4:1-11 NKJV

The devil approached Jesus three times in the text that we just read. Every time the devil spoke he twisted the truth of the Word of God. This is an epic encounter between two kings. One is the King of Lies and the other is the King of Kings but the King of Lies speaks, twists and alters the truth. The King of Kings answers those lies. He doesn't simply answer with an idea or a philosophy, He answered with the Word of God! He says, "It is written." If we are going to be effective in combating the lies of the devil we must become familiar with what is written.

Let's be like Jesus and resist the lies of the enemy! The Devil has stolen too many marriages and too many families with his lies. It is a perfect time to become an, **"IT IS WRITTEN"** kind of person! Answer every lie with the scripture. It is a powerful tool to drive back lying thoughts and attacks from the enemy. The truth of God will overcome any lie from the Devil, so let's destroy the lies.

LOVE HANDLE:

Identify a lie in your life. Find a scripture that obliterates it. Use that scripture this week to change that mindset. Repeat the truth as many times as you can. Now commit to following this same pattern every time you detect a lie in your life.

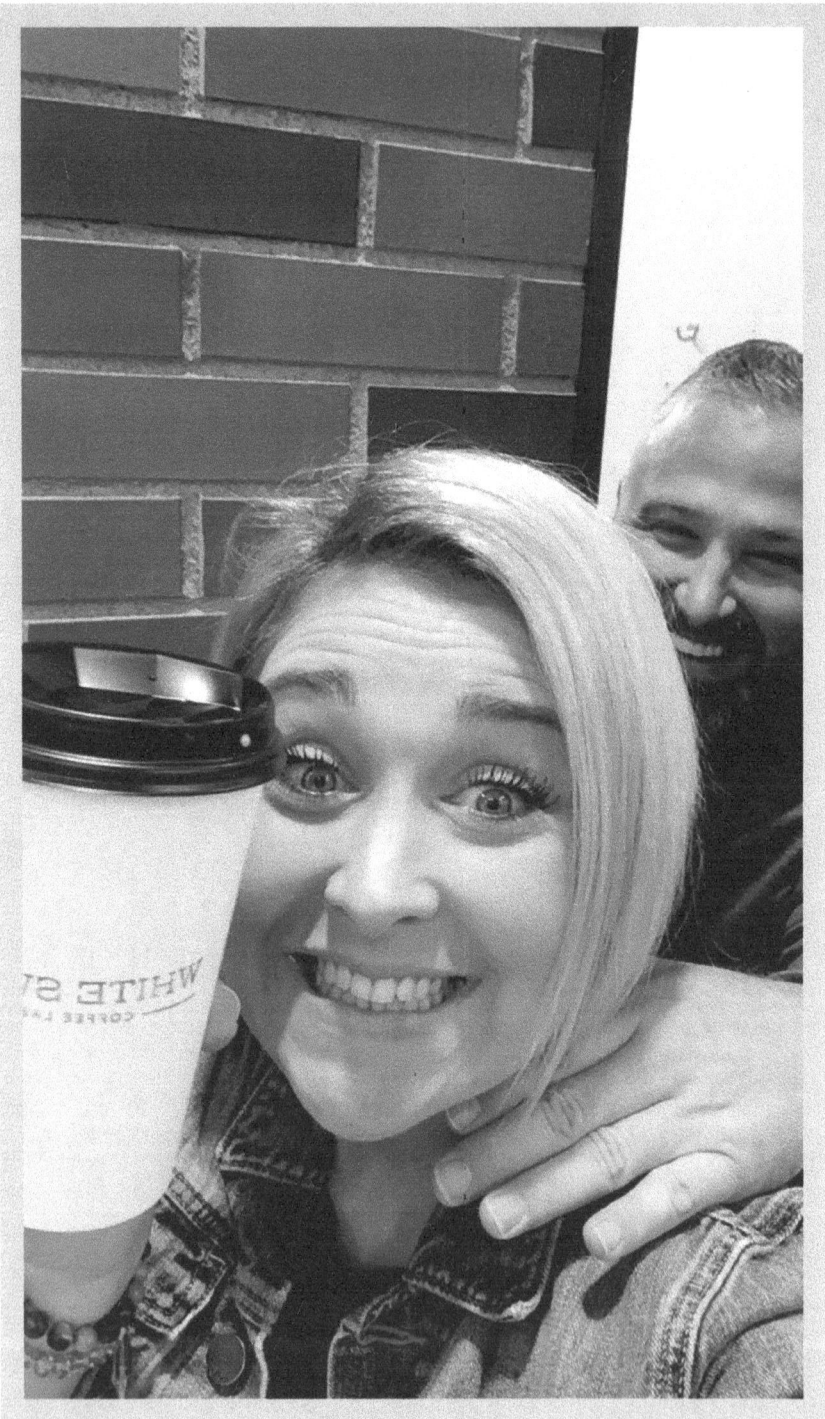

CHAPTER 6:

LOVE HANDLES COMMUNICATION

"Death and life are in the power of the tongue, And those who love it will eat its fruit." Proverbs 18:21 NKJV

COMMUNICATION CAN MAKE YOU OR BREAK YOU!

"RECENTLY, JESSI AND I WERE PREPARING TO GIVE A SERIES OF MARRIAGE TALKS TO A CONGREGATION OF PEOPLE."

We do this kind of speaking frequently on various subjects. Every year we do a full month of marriage teaching for His Church (the church that we Pastor). I always know when we get ready to teach on this topic that our marriage will be challenged!

I was helping one of my daughters do her math homework (I don't remember junior high math being this difficult!). I looked at one of her problems and could tell that she had simply guessed on one of her answers. I began to explain to my daughter how guessing will simply not work in the field of mathematics. I learned through my many years in education that there are some subjects that you can "fake it till you make it," but math is not one of them. I looked at her and said, "Guessing will do you no good in math!"

I then walked to the back of the house where Jessi was getting ready. She looked at me when I walked into the room and said, "Do you want to fight or something?" I responded, "What do you mean?" She said, "I heard what you said, 'Jessi does not help me at all in life!' ' I immediately started laughing and told her what I actually said! We both almost fell over laughing! Can you see how communication can make you or break you?

How many couples are out there trying to create a dream marriage but they simply are not hearing what the other person is saying? How many people don't know how to communicate what they are feeling to their spouse? How many marriages end due to the lack of communication? I believe that God wants our marriages to thrive. He wants to give you a Love Handle to grab ahold of in this area and I believe if we learn to communicate well we can learn to do marriage well. You can start really hearing what the other person is saying.

My two decades of Christian leadership have taught me that most men learn to communicate through a series of growls, grunts, sighs, and screams. Many males find it extremely difficult to express themselves except in moments of anger. Then they say way too much at the wrong time and damage those they love the most. Many women also have a very hard time communicating what they are actually feeling. Communication isn't simply a male or a female issue, it is a human issue. Learning to communicate effectively takes work and it is a lifelong endeavor, but if you learn to communicate well it will pay huge dividends.

UNDER COMMUNICATOR

Most people will fall into the category of under communication for the things that really count. They might even be great with words and small talk. I have met many people who could light up the room during a meet and greet time, but could not communicate to their spouse about the things that really mattered. The person who cannot communicate often lives in a frustrated world because they have expectations of their spouse that are unreal. These expectations are unreal because they have never been communicated. The spouse of the under communicator lives in a world of guesswork because they have never been told what their spouse really expects of them. The under communicator will say things like, "If you don't know by now" and "You should have figured it out."

I was raised by a father who was a great man but a classic under-communicator! His mode of communication was to send a message to us through our mother. We would then decipher the message and respond back to our father through our mother. I have often jokingly called her the Holy Spirit in our household. The Holy Spirit in the Bible is the one who shows us what the Father is saying. When Jessi and I were newly married I was good at communication because I am, by nature and occupation, a speaker. However, I was not good at communicating about what really mattered and I had to develop that part of my life.

If you are the under communicator you most likely know that I am writing about you by now. If not I'm sure your spouse does. It's okay to be turned that way but it is not okay to stay that way! That attitude is the kiss of death to a marriage. To have a great marriage we must all be willing to work on ourselves. Jessi and I make it a priority once a week to look at each other and ask some hard questions. Those questions are things like, "Do you still like me?" Sometimes the answers are, "I like you just not this week!"

I have to credit Jessi for forcing me to communicate on an ongoing basis early in marriage. It really set us up for success as a married couple. What the under communicator needs is a system that forces them to communicate on a consistent basis. Set up a weekly time for real communication. Make a list of topics that need to be discussed: sexual fulfillment, financial communication, romantic desires, areas that need help. Often just the communication itself will bring health to that area of your marriage.

OVER COMMUNICATORS

It's funny how time can change the environment that you live in. I was raised with a bunch of under communicators but now I live in a world of over communicators! Both Jessi and I have been speaking for our entire adult lives occupationally. Our children have it in their DNA! When the five of us get in a car together someone is always talking. Typically three people are talking at a time. I have had other people ride with us and they ask, "Is it always like this?" We tell them that we used to have secrets but now we have children. Our children tell it, tell it often, and tell it all!

The over communicator lives in a different world than the under communicator. This person has to learn the art of discretion and self-control. The Bible is full of warnings concerning using words loosely.

> "A fool vents all his feelings, But a wise man holds them back."
> Proverbs 29:11 NKJV

The over communicator must remember that life and death are in the power of the tongue. They can communicate their concerns, but they must remember that people can only handle so much perceived correction at a time. If a spouse starts to think that communication has morphed into character assassination they will shut you down quickly. The over communicator must continually remind themselves to tell it, but don't tell it all, and don't tell it all the time! If they begin to tell it all the time they can fall into the biblical category of the fool - venting all their feelings. Remember we are after clear and edifying communication, not just getting something off our chests. Getting something off our chests can simply put it on our spouse's shoulders.

> "Therefore, putting away lying, " Let each one of you speak truth with his neighbor," for we are members of one another."Be angry, and do not sin": do not let the sun go down on your wrath, nor give place to the devil. Let him who stole steal no longer, but rather let him labor, working with his hands, which is good, that he may have something to give him who has need. Let no corrupt word proceed out of your mouth, but what is good for necessary edification, that it may impart grace to the hearers. And do not grieve the Holy Spirit of God, by whom you were sealed for the day of redemption. Let all bitterness, wrath, anger, clamor, and evil speaking be put away from you, with all malice. And be kind to one another, tenderhearted, forgiving one another, even as God in Christ forgave you." Ephesians 4:25-32 NKJV

Communication is a massive part of the human experience. It's an even larger part of marriage. Our experience as Pastors over the last nineteen years has taught us that the people who learn to communicate with each other are the people who thrive in marriage.

The Apostle Paul writes about the importance of Christian communication in the text above! He tells us to:

- Speak the truth.
- Avoid corrupt communication.
- Build others up with our speech.
- Use our words to bring grace.
- Put away evil speaking.

He also talks about grieving the Holy Spirit in this portion of scripture. It's a whole portion of scriptures that deals with the way we communicate. I believe that our communication can bring grief to the Holy Spirit, that is how powerful our words really are. They can actually bring grief to God, Himself!

If our words are so powerful that they can have an effect on God, they certainly will have an effect on our spouse, our children, and the people that we love. I want my words to build my spouse up, not break my spouse down. Let's find the time to communicate wisely. You can learn the art of communication. It's a love handle that you grab hold of. When you strengthen that communication you will develop a marriage so strong that it will stand the test of time.

Jessi learned a counseling technique years ago at college that I believe can help the hard communication cases. It's a technique that involves standing on a rug. The person that is standing on the rug has the floor. It is their time to express their feelings, concerns, and opinions. After they finish with their time on the rug the other person gets the rug. That person must now repeat what their spouse just said back to them until they agree that they understood what they were saying. Only after this, can the second spouse begin to communicate their needs, wants, wishes, and desires. It is a technique that can be a great blessing in the area of communication.

LOVE HANDLE:

- Have a time scheduled that you communicate.
- Lower your voice.
- Remember that your spouse needs to be heard.
- Remember that your spouse needs to hear you.
- Work until you get it done.
- Use the rug.

A great focus for the under communicator is to schedule a weekly time when you clearly communicate on topics that are uncomfortable. Be sure to schedule this at a time when you are most rested and not distracted. Then keep your appointment.

A great focus for the over communicator may be to write down what you will focus on. Be sure to have a plan and do not "wing it" even if you feel confident that you can. Do not allow the communication to become a character assassination.

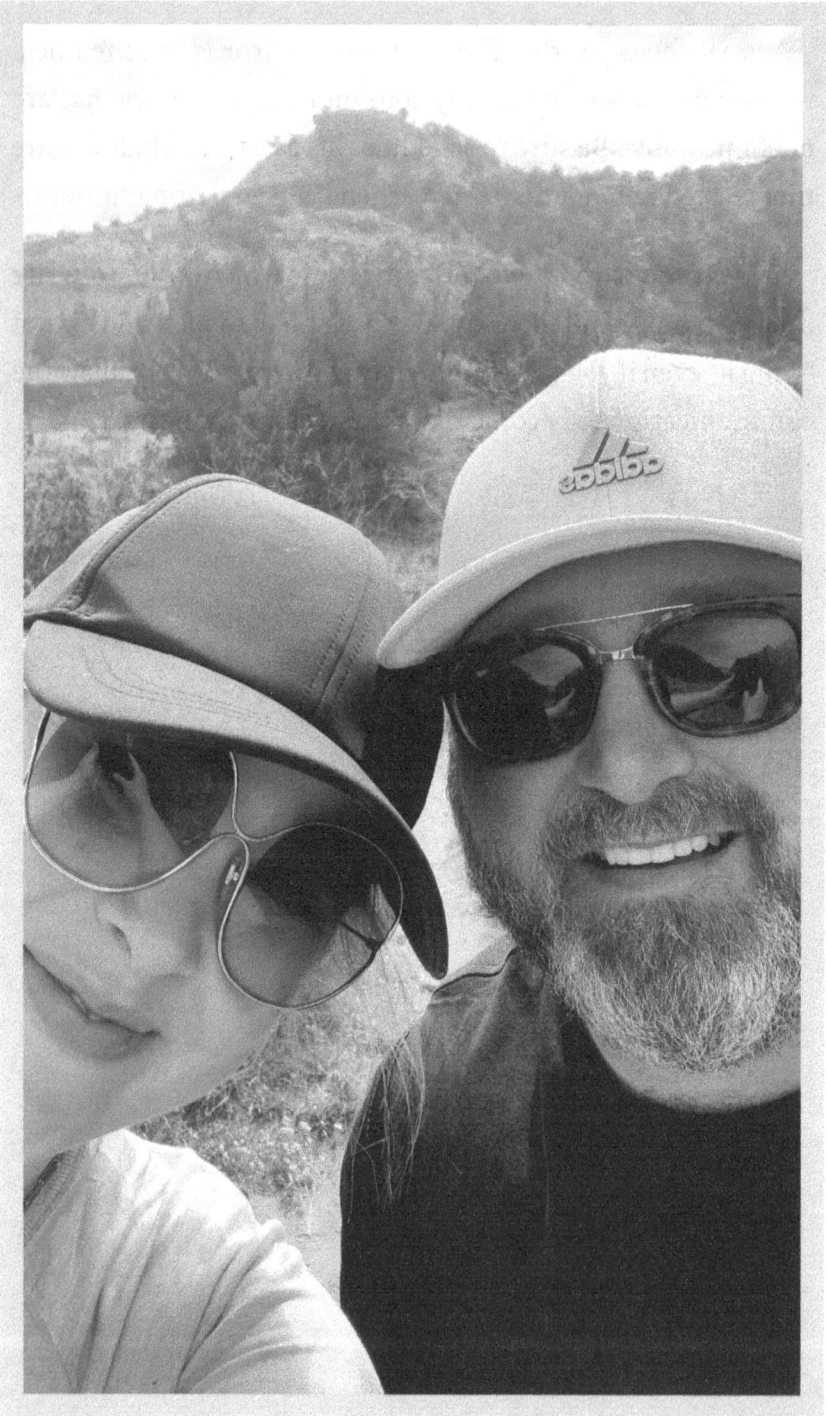

CHAPTER 7:

LOVE HANDLES SEX

"Marriage is honorable among all, and the bed undefiled; but fornicators and adulterers God will judge."
Hebrews 13:4 NKJV

"SEX MATTERS. WAIT A MINUTE— THAT IS AN UNDERSTATEMENT—SEX MATTERS BIG-TIME."

Wait a minute—that is still a massive understatement—sex matters in a super, massive, ginormous, big-time way. **Sex, money, and communication are all make or break issues in the marriage.** It's funny how we have a world that's become so super sexual but when it comes to sex and marriage the majority of Christians want to be quiet about it.

The world that we live in is certainly working overtime to paint a picture of sexuality. Think about the songs on pop radio, the theme is almost always sex. It's all about that bass,

She's a brick house, Let me see that Tootsie Roll, Let's Get It On, Baby Got Back, Don't You Wish Your Girlfriend Was Hot Like Me, etc. Pop radio has practically become soft porn! Every advertisement that you see is based on sexuality, even burgers are sold with sexual imagery. Nothing is off-limits.

News anchors are prettier than ever and football isn't exciting enough without the cheerleaders. We now need every commercial to include sexualization. Have you ever noticed that people are beautiful!? Why is it like this? It's because sex captures our attention and we are created to be sexual creatures. Because of this, sex sells. So sex has been selling beer, clothing, food, and a million other lifestyle products for decades. In the midst of all of this selling, God's message about sex and marriage has been lost.

You can discover just how lost God's message about sexuality in marriage is in pop culture by listening to the things people say before someone gets married. They make it sound as if the best days of your sex life are behind you when in all actuality they should be beginning. Pop culture has shown us this picture of life that has sexual experience, freedom, and fulfillment before marriage, but after marriage, it suggests that the party is over.

There was a reality TV series released recently that entailed people having their marriage pre-arranged by experts. I thought it was an interesting social experiment. Religion, preference, race, and even living standards were taken into account during the matching process, they found a mate for each person that they thought had the best chance of being successful. During this show, the big "plot twist" seemed to be a virgin being matched up with a man. I was excited to see how thrilled he would be that she had decided to give a gift to her husband that very few men get when they marry a girl. I was shocked to see him be disappointed.

He was clearly concerned and even let down that she had no experience. He explained that it was a lot of responsibility and he didn't feel he was the right man for her. He ultimately chose to not stay with her even though he adored everything else about her because he didn't want someone inexperienced. I was shocked that this man would have preferred that his wife give her body to men and get sexual "experience".

Pornography has not only become the norm amongst men and women statistically but it is growing as we become more and more perverse as a culture. Great sex as God intended between a husband and wife after marriage vows is so abnormal that people almost seem repulsed by the thought of it. This is not what God intended. He intended men to "Rejoice in the wife of their youth" and wanted them to "Let her breasts satisfy you all the days of your life". We are created to enter our peak sexuality and the greatest sexual season the day we say "I do."

Our culture sees dating as a time to gain such experience and marriage as the time when the well dries up over time. The more weddings we do the more I realize that this is not a standard mindset in our nation. Moms, dads, uncles, aunts, and friends are standing around after rehearsal dinners begging young people not to throw their best sexual years away. When young people decide to marry they are told that their life as they know it is over. Groomsmen are in corners with Grandfathers laughing about what a fool the groom is, and how he will regret rushing into a monogamous marriage. That is not at all the way God intended our marriage to be!

God designed us to be sexual. He created marriage between a man and a woman to fulfill that desire. His design was for two people to grow in their knowledge of one another and each other's bodies. He intended the bond of friendship and partnership to drive the sexual desire for one another, and for that bond to deepen over time. Decades and decades of dedicated study of what makes one person happy is best. Two people making each other's physical body a priority, and even a hobby, was the perfect plan of God.

In this place, a couple is not only equally physically fulfilled (notice both people are fulfilled) but also emotionally, and yes even spiritually, because when God designs something for us He does it perfectly and we engage in an activity that isn't just natural. The marriage is where all the hot stuff is supposed to happen! **Christian marriage is supposed to be full of mind-blowing, toe-curling, and scream-out loud, sex!**

—Pastor Brian Gibson

SEX IS POWERFUL

Sex is a powerful tool. One might say that sex is power. It's a force so powerful that it literally creates life.

It's also a force so powerful that we've all seen it destroy life. Let's think about the life-creating power of sex. Right now you're reading this book; You have a body, spirit, and soul. You are the most complex organism on the planet, a living being created in the image of God. How did you get here? The answer is simple – sex!

Sex has the power to create a human being. It also has the power to create a life-giving relationship within the bounds of marriage. God created sex to strengthen the marriage covenant and it is an intimacy that's to be shared between a man and his wife. What a powerful privilege! To really know someone and to be known by them. To know every detail will take years, not a one-night stand. Conversations about likes and dislikes and not just arguments about deficiency or lack of frequency. It will require time and attention and a lot of giving without thinking of yourself for periods of time. It requires stopping the world of activity and ignoring the television and phone.

Great sex as God intended it requires A LOT but the bond that comes from this kind of intentionality cannot be replicated or had by those who are not willing to put in the effort. Contrary to public opinion. A person is not born with the skills needed to fulfill a single person sexually for life. If you will acquire this skill you must create a bond that can only be acquired in a covenant. Inside of this covenant relationship, sex helps create such a bond. Anyone can have sex, but only people that follow God's map can have the kind of sex that God intended, and it is anything but "regular" or "old".

Sex is also a force that can be destructive. We've all heard of high-risk sexual behavior. That's a term that describes someone's actions who hasn't really counted the cost of toying with the power of sex. As a Pastor and someone who helps people on the days the bombs drop in their life I've seen the destructive nature of sexual immorality first hand.

You start to realize that sex is a force and not a toy when someone tells you that the test is positive for HIV. You start to realize that sex is a force and not a toy when a husband sits in your office so confused and angry that your heart breaks as he realizes that the baby in his wife's womb, that he thought was his flesh and blood, could definitely belong to another man. All the while, his other children are at home knowing that something is desperately wrong but unsure why their home feels scary and unsure. That family altered forever is a great reminder of the power of sex used as a toy. You definitely get it when the whole family is weeping in your office due to a pregnant 15-year-old girl. All delusions about sex leave you in these times. It's crazy how something that can start life can also stop life.

BOUNDARIES BRING SAFETY:

One of the greatest ways to bring safety to your sex life is to agree to Biblical boundaries and stick to them.

Never bring anyone else into your bedroom. Whether they are in person or on the screen, it will not "spice anything up". It will bring destruction and it will leave you empty.

- Never harm your spouse.
- Never do anything that convicts your spouse.
- The marriage bed is undefiled (aka have a blast).

These are spiritually sound boundaries that we are commanded to keep from scripture.

We can also use practical tips for a successful sex life!

HAVE SEX REGULARLY

"Do not deprive each other except perhaps by mutual consent and for a time, so that you may devote yourselves to prayer. Then come together again so that Satan will not tempt you because of your lack of self-control."
I Corinthians 7:5 NKJV

The Bible clearly lays out the danger of not regularly having sex when married. We are called to be faithful to one another. Notice you are only allowed to deprive your spouse for prolonged times of prayer (not just because you want to hold them hostage). Having sex regularly can be hard for some for different reasons but it is our job to communicate through life seasons, sickness, family distress, work schedules, hormone changes, business demands and regularly experience this sexual connection. Even scripture understands that this puts the faithfulness of marriage in danger due to the nature of human beings. God created us to have regular sexual encounters. He never intended us to go long periods of time without the release and connection this act brings into the marriage relationship.

When we teach on this subject in our church every year Brian started telling people to have sex every day. He was making a humorous point that if you did this most people wouldn't have the energy to have an affair. People would laugh and we would move on to actually instruct them scripturally how important it is to have sex regularly.

Apparently, word got around about this statement but no one explained the humor that was attached so now there is a salon I cannot walk into in our community without the stylists shouting "Hey guys it's the sex everyday lady"! No matter how many times I try to explain myself and the intent of this comment, it makes no difference in my reception. I'm used to it now and we all get a good laugh every time it happens.

Obviously, this isn't humanly possible for most people in the real world and it is a joke, but as Pastors we see the couple's that war with sex. They use it as a weapon or refuse to have it for six months and then act shocked when they find out their spouse stepped outside the marriage to have sex. Nothing makes the affair ok, but in most of these cases, it could have been avoided if the couple would just heed the words in Corinthians. Let's face it, if we are honest, we didn't get married to not have sex. I want to offer a word of warning. If you don't, somebody else will! No doubt about that. There are people that are willing and waiting at every turn to tempt and pursue your spouse. Do not allow temptation to sneak in. Have sex and pray for God to give your spouse wisdom to see the temptation and also the way of escape every time!

REGULARITY OVER ROMANCE

Don't get me wrong. I like romance as much as the next girl. A perfect night with sweet and thoughtful things is wonderful and needed, lingerie is great and roses and candles are special but do yourself a favor, don't wait.

Let yourself enjoy your spouse regularly. On a normal day. In the middle of the chaos of toddlers. After a day of T-ball when the kitchen isn't cleaned up from your fast food failure of a healthy meal. Let yourself off the hook of perfection and I promise you that at the end of your life you will be so glad that you did. You won't look at your spouse at eighty-five and say every sexual encounter we had looked like a movie and that made me happy. That will mean you probably only had sex twice. Let your spouse love you just like you are. Don't wait until you've had a pedicure or fixed your hair. Don't wait until you lose twenty pounds and, please, whatever you do, don't wait until the kids are gone to grandma's. Just enjoy one another.

Sex is the perfect hobby and it's free. You can have it when you are broke or wealthy. You can enjoy each other while fighting to build a life, and after you have created that life. Let it become a hobby and look forward to it. Study it and read books that make you good at it. No matter how many years you have under your notched belt, you should never underestimate how important a good study of human anatomy or a documentary on human sexuality, and how it pertains to the body of your spouse, can be.

Listen to find what you can learn and not just try to write down tips for your spouse. Be quick to ask for things you need and slow to criticize the actions that you already encountered. Never give up on learning or think that you understand it fully. No matter what you think, you're probably not as good at it as you think you are. Believe us, your spouse sent a note asking us to write this chapter!

—Pastor Jessi Gibson

"I'VE HEARD SEX DESCRIBED
AS DYNAMITE."

That's a funny term, sexual dynamite. That's what I'm gonna make Jessi start calling me. Ha! The reason that people compare sex to dynamite is because of its nature. Sex, like dynamite, is explosive and that explosion can be used to do something positive. Dynamite can be used to mine precious metals out of the ground. Explosives have been used to put gold, diamonds, silver, and fossil fuels in the hands of human beings for centuries. These explosives are powerful. Dynamite, when handled inappropriately, can end someone's life. I was raised in a coal mining area of the country. The majority of the men from my community worked in underground mines and used high-powered explosives in their work. If those explosives were mishandled people died. It's just like sex, and for sex to be a blessing, not a burden, we must understand its nature. If you don't get a hold of this love handle your marriage will become a ticking time bomb.

SEX CONNECTS

Sex is given to us for reproduction. God told Adam and Eve in the Garden of Eden to multiply and fill up the earth. God wants righteous families on the earth, but I don't believe that's the only reason that God gave us sex. He gave us sex as a tool to connect us! When the book of Genesis starts defining marriage it uses the term, "one flesh."

> "Therefore a man shall leave his father
> and mother and be joined to his wife,
> and they shall become one flesh. And
> they were both naked, the man and his
> wife, and were not ashamed."
> Genesis 2:24-25 NKJV

Marriage is the most powerful union on earth. God describes that union as a "one flesh" experience. God made us male and female to join us together spiritually, relationally, emotionally, and physically. When you get married you are no longer two separate people, but you become one. Sex itself is a physical action that is a perfect picture of what has happened spiritually between a man and his wife. Sex within the bounds of marriage is the strongest connection that is possible between two people. Sex is a tool that connects us.

Sex connects us in such a deep and spiritual way that it's hard to explain with words alone. This is why the new American model of dating and marriage brings so much pain to so many people. We have told our young people not to get married early in life. Wait a while, live a little, sow your wild oats! We have now created a culture where people are putting off marriage until their thirties and even forties. Parents especially on the coastlines of America are starting to look more like grandparents than parents. This type of thinking has also invaded the church. The one thing that has not been considered with this type of mindset is the reality of a set of Christian sexual ethics.

When we tell people to wait, don't get married, and spend their twenties on themselves, we are effectively telling them to sleep with everyone who will hold still for them for a decade! This creates a cycle of pain. Whenever two people join themselves together in a sexual union there is a real connection. When these two people part ways there is a tearing apart of that connection that causes pain and sets them up for failure in life. God's laws about sex and marriage aren't to stop you from having fun. They're designed to protect you from disease, heartbreak, and emotional pain.

It breaks my heart to see young people going from relationship to relationship. They're often trying to fulfill the need for companionship in their lives. So they jump from relationship to relationship because they aren't ready to settle down yet. After all, they have bought into the American dating lie. They have what I call multiple mini-marriages before they actually say I do. Then they bring the pain and the baggage of all these previous relationships into their marriage.

When they have these pretend, mini-marriages, they inevitably end up with a sexual relationship. That sexual relationship creates a deep connection between these two people, and when they part ways, a scar is left. A scar that they will carry into their marriage.

This kind of lifestyle is divorce practice. It makes the heart more and more callous every time they rip away from a deep relationship and by the time they finally marry, it's so easy to just divorce if they find themselves unhappy at any point.

It's typically a sex drive that brings a couple together in the first place and that is divine design, it's how it works. People get to a point in their life where they are single and ready to mingle! They get hot to trot, the need to breed or the urge to merge. At this point in life, a person's attention heads towards the opposite sex. They start looking for someone to fulfill these desires in their life. Most relationships don't start off with love; they begin because someone is in heat.

I have to admit that the first time I saw Jessi I wasn't drawn to her Christlike character or her amazing intellect. I was drawn to the fact that I walked into a room and she was on a Healthrider. A Healthrider was a 1990's exercise machine that required you to grab a hold of a bar and make a thrusting motion to work out your core. She had me from hello! I know it sounds like I was a dirty old man but nothing could be further from the truth. I was a healthy, normal, and extremely excited twenty-year-old man! Sex drive was a tool that God used to put me with the right person. Now I don't want you to think that we gave in quickly to our desires. Jessi already had her youth ministry where she taught teenagers about sexual abstinence until marriage. She took a vow before God that she would not even kiss a man until she stood at the marriage altar. To get the girl I had to hold my horses.

Even though we wanted to do things our own way, we decided to do what God asked. It wasn't easy. We were tempted, we hated engagement and wanted to come together but we did pull the reins and do what God asked of us. We just made the engagement short! "It's better to marry than to burn with passion" is in the Bible for a reason, right?

Needless to say, it was worth it all. We now see clearly on the other side. We see that God commands abstinence so trust can be built and pain can be avoided. He asks us to wait so we will know that our spouse has self-control. If they obey God when they want you the most, it will be easier to trust that they will obey Him again and again throughout your marriage, even when you age, wrinkle, change, gain weight, lose hair, etc.

It is in those seasons that you will need to know they have the self-control needed to abstain, even when they might want someone other than you, or be tempted by someone else. This time of engagement is the perfect time to set up a lifetime of trust! Encourage the young people in your life to use it for good and not let it pass by just picking out flowers or the perfect gown. It matters in every season.

It may even be a good idea to talk with your spouse if you were not knowledgeable in this area or you didn't bat one hundred percent during this season. It's never too late to ask them to just simply forgive you and then, together, ask God to help renew that if He hasn't already.

Some people naturally go through this transition but others desperately need healing in this area so they can move out of jealousy and strife. This is a root that needs to be pulled out, and this happens through repentance and forgiveness. The lack of faithfulness that people experience in their marriages isn't just against them personally, it is actually rooted in a lack of faithfulness to God's commands. It isn't as personal as it is spiritual. So, if you have struggled in your marriage with these things, stop now and do the work that it takes to walk in forgiveness, trust, faithfulness, and wholeness. Your marriage and family depend on your willingness to listen to God's command and follow it even if you feel you are years too late. God redeems time and

He does miracles. This may be the first moment that you have realized what the root of your issue is and this is your moment to fix it! Don't move on until you take the time to repent.

—Pastor Brian Gibson

LOVE HANDLE:

Take five minutes to think about your pre-married commitment to God's commands of abstinence and sexual purity. If you have anything to repent for, do it now. Don't wait. God is listening. If you need to ask your spouse to forgive you so that trust can grow, DO IT!! The only better day was yesterday.

CHAPTER 8:

LOVE HANDLES MONEY

"Honor the LORD with your possessions, And with the firstfruits of all your increase; So your barns will be filled with plenty, And your vats will overflow with new wine." Proverbs 3:9-10 NKJV

"I REMEMBER THE CHANCELLOR OF THE UNIVERSITY WE GRADUATED FROM USED TO SAY, "THE THINGS THAT WILL DESTROY A MAN ARE THE GOLD, THE GIRLS, AND THE GLORY."

He was talking to young preachers. He could've also said it like this – the things that will destroy a man or a woman are money, sex and power. Those words still ring true. How many times have we seen this scenario play out? These topics repeat again and again in news cycles, movies, and family issues. These same issues haunt marriages - Money,

Sex, and Power. Instead of money being something that destroys, it can be a blessing. You can honor the Lord with it!

In this chapter, I want to address the topic of money. I want you to keep this in mind - money is not a bad thing! I believe that it is a good thing. I can hear the questions coming, "But Pastor, doesn't the Bible say that money is the root of all evil?" No, it never says that. That is a scripture that has been misquoted since the beginning of time. What was actually written was this:

> "For the love of money is a root of all kinds of evil, for which some have strayed from the faith in their greediness, and pierced themselves through with many sorrows."
> I Timothy 6:10 NKJV

What Paul was telling his young disciple Timothy was that the love of money is the root of all evil. He never said that the money itself was the root of evil. Money is something that every couple will need. We need it to feed our families, to house ourselves, to clothe our children, etc.

Most husbands and wives are going to spend forty plus hours a week in the pursuit of money. We live in a culture that typically requires two incomes to make ends meet. Both husbands and wives are busy during the week in the pursuit of money. How we spend that money can become a major point of controversy in a marriage and as a Pastor, I've seen marriages taken out over money issues.

I believe that many of these money issues are developed long before a couple says I do. Many of the opinions people form about money come from their childhood years. They watch mom or dad fight about money, or freak out about money, but never really teach them how to use it as a proper tool to push their lives forward. How many of you can remember taking a practical class about money in high school? It didn't exist when I was in school. In most houses money was a taboo topic that kids aren't supposed to bring up.

Now you take two young people and bind them in an eternal covenant. They are married now, till death do us part! They both have some sort of opinion about money, but most of the time they are somewhat different opinions. This is where a little premarital counseling can go a very, very long way. I've seen supersavers marry super spenders. I've seen aggressive investors married to people who are frightened to start a snow cone stand! Let's face it, whenever most of us were newly married we knew next to nothing about money. It takes time for people to develop a financial flow that causes them to work as a team.

IT'S NO LONGER YOUR MONEY!

I walked by and noticed a photograph from our wedding day recently. I look like I've been dragged behind a truck for the last twenty years! Jessi still looks the same. On the day that we became one, everything that Jessi owned became mine, and everything that I owned became Jessi's. The Bible says the two shall become one flesh. I believe that spiritually, I believe it physically, I believe it financially! Whenever we first got married also we were so young I took Jessi on a honeymoon to Disney World (before we knew what we now know about the Disney organization). We had the time of our lives. I can remember it like it was yesterday, we stayed at their Polynesian resort and then for a night or two in the Grand Floridian. I remember some kids in the park thought that Jessi was Snow White. Let's just say she doesn't spend a lot of time tanning! We spent the whole week at Disney World and then Jessi came to me one night and said, "I forgot my belt." She could barely keep her shorts up. I said to her, "Well, why didn't you just buy one?" She looked at me in disbelief. It never crossed her mind that she could buy a new belt.

It was a revelation to me of how different we have been raised in our thinking about money. Her parents have been Pastors living on a limited salary, my parents have been business people that made great money. I never had to worry or think about my clothes or any other financial hardship coming up. My wife's childhood had been quite different. We had two different mindsets that God was going to have to take and form into one household.

With my upbringing I watched my family learn how to make money. They worked hard and they worked long hours. From the time I was big enough not to be killed by cattle, I worked for my family in the Livestock business. We've worked so hard, it was one of the greatest gifts my parents ever gave me. Work ethic is something I was taught to value deeply, but because my family worked hard and made a lot of money they also spent rather freely. I remember going to the mall with my mom to pick out clothes. Whatever was on the mannequin was what I wore at home. It turned me into a spender!

Jessi's father was raising a family of five on a Pastor's salary of an upstart charismatic church in the 1980's. Jessi's parents worked with what they had and worked very hard, long hours as Pastors. Like many ministers, they made great sacrifices to preach the gospel of Jesus Christ of Nazareth. Jessi and her sisters were taught to stretch a dollar as far as they could and to be frugal. In her childhood, she remembers getting clothes on special occasions. She would receive things like that on her birthday, Christmas, and back to school. By nature, she was being trained to be a saver more than a spender.

I must admit that my spending habits have probably bothered Jessi at times in our marriage. Cash on hand is not something that I've ever placed great value upon.

I've always loved investing but cash in an account has always seemed like something to get me to a goal, the next project, or an investment. Jessi on the other hand sees great security in having cash on hand in the bank. I know that she's right about having these holdings but I've always hated seeing money that was sitting in an account and not making money. As our marriage has progressed we've learned to compromise. I keep enough cash on hand to make her comfortable and she allows me the freedom to speculate and invest when opportunities arise.

Every couple will have some form of financial disagreement. It may be the amount of money that they are willing to spend on a house. It may be over buying a used or a new car. It may be over a clothing allowance or a piece of jewelry, but I promise you one thing, a financial disagreement is coming! The best thing that you can do to be ready for these financial disagreements is to set some ground rules. I'm not gonna give you a right or a wrong way for you to run the finances of your home. There are many books that you can read about financial management. What I would like to do is give you some ideas that will help the two of you clarify your financial goals and concerns.

Both spouses should write out their clear financial goals and say them out loud to the other spouse to make sure there's a clear understanding. That spouse should repeat what they said back to them.

Both spouses should know exactly where the house is financially at least once a month if not weekly. You don't want to get old and learn in your vulnerable years that your spouse never took care of your retirement.

Both spouses should view the finances as ours and not mine. It's okay to have separate accounts for separate purposes but the money must be viewed as ours.

I believe that if a couple will come into agreement about their finances, the blessing of God will flood into their material lives. God is looking for couples that he can invest His resources into that will take care of His church! I believe that you can be one of those couples. If we will honor the principles that are recorded in the word of God by moving in Biblical generosity and management it will be crazy to see how God blesses you!"

—Pastor Brian Gibson

LOVE HANDLE:

Take a little time this week to set goals. What is important to you? Set a specific time to discuss what is important to both of you based on this information and come together on a plan to be unified in your financial life.

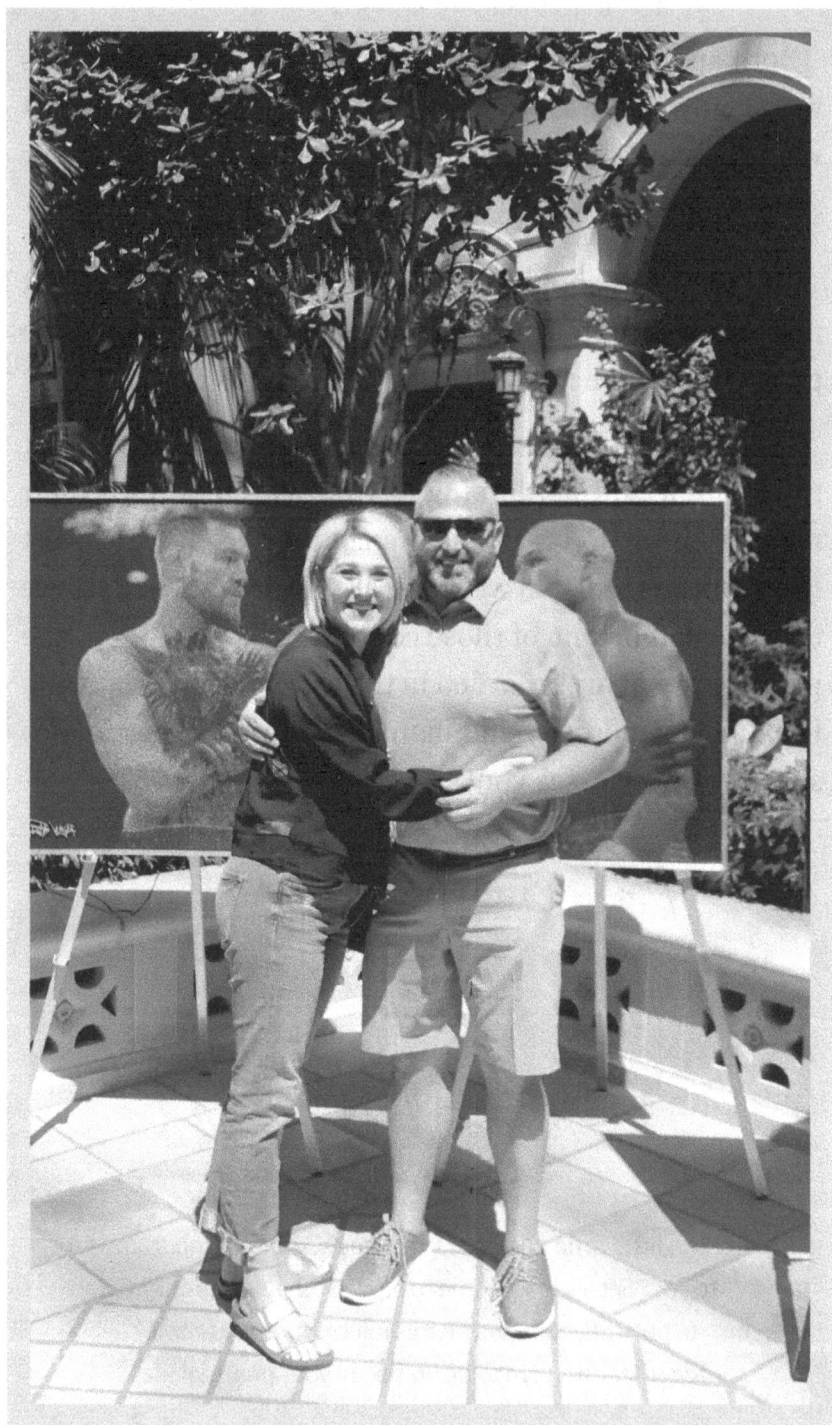

CHAPTER 9:

LOVE HANDLES HURT

"He heals the brokenhearted and binds
up their wounds." Psalms 147:3 NKJV

"LET'S TALK FOR A MOMENT ABOUT WHAT MARRIAGE IS REALLY LIKE! IT'S A PARTNERSHIP, THE DEEPEST AND MOST FULFILLING PARTNERSHIP ON THE EARTH."

With a partnership, you have real help in life! The partnership brings another mind, intellect, skill set, resource, and work ethic into the equation of your life. It also brings another person. A person that you are sworn to be with "until death do us part", for the good times and the bad times, the mountains and the valleys.

Jessi and I have had some of the greatest times imaginable! We've had three beautiful children. We've had the privilege of pioneering and Pastoring a great church that has now spread to multiple locations. We've traveled the world together preaching the Word of God. We had the great privilege of fundraising for safe homes for children who have been rescued from sex trafficking. It's been an incredible two decades.

We have also had some of the worst times imaginable. We live in a fallen world, the earth after original sin, is a crash site. Things don't always go as planned. The story doesn't always end the way that you would like it to. There are real injuries and real losses. Some seasons in life are real tests. Thank God for the partnership of marriage to get us through the testing times of life. Life has a way of hurting people. You have to be prepared and make a decision about how you are going to handle the tough times.

I learned a lot about handling tough times from my mother. She is five feet tall, a true lady, and tough as nails. She was always sweet to me as a child. I still think that I am her favorite. I am the baby of the family, and we babies typically believe that we are special! However in my mother's mind, there was no such thing as sick days. She had too much to do to lay down. She was raising three boys and running a business. She knew that to win in life you couldn't lay down.

Because of this, we had to produce a high-grade fever to miss school. I'm talking like a nuclear heat on your body, or a life-threatening illness! I would say that I felt bad and she would send me on to school and out to work in the family business. It made a man out of me and it kept me going through the tough times in marriage and life. My mother recently had a heart attack (she got through it without any real damage) and that afternoon she was trying to arrange to watch my kids the next day! Her attitude is, "It's just a little heart attack, put some tape on it and get back in the game!" We were able to talk her into resting because we needed her to be better so she could stay around for those same kids for a long time. For some people it is hard to decipher whether we are hurt or injured. There is a difference."

— Pastor Brian Gibson

ARE YOU HURT OR INJURED?

"The LORD is near to those who have a broken heart, And saves such as have a contrite spirit." Psalms 34:18 NKJV

"I'm thankful for high school coaches. I really believe that they push young men and women beyond themselves to expand their limits. Almost anyone who has played competitive sports has had an experience like this one. I can remember playing high school football and getting my socks rocked. Someone nailed me and knocked the breath out of me, I never saw them coming! I was on my back and not getting up. As the coach came and hovered over me. I heard him say, "Gibson, are you hurt or are you injured?"

I thought to myself, both! It took me a while to figure out what he was talking about.

Hurt for a football player is something like a broken finger. It's uncomfortable and painful but it's not a game-stopping injury. You go to the sidelines and put some tape on it and finish the game. It's just a broken finger, you'll live, you have nine more of them. Injured is another story. Injured is when the ligaments in your knee are torn and moved out of place. You can't stand up or catch your breath and all you can feel is pain. There is no finishing the game and your night ends with an ambulance ride.

The people who do well in marriage learn to play hurt. Life has a way of hurting you but you can rise above it. You must learn to play with the pain. Many people walk out of marriages because they are hurt but not really injured. If they only would have learned to play hurt their family would still be together. Many people walk out of churches because they are hurt but not injured. People give up on dreams because they are hurt but they are not injured. An injured man might not be able to finish the game but a hurt man can. You need to ask yourself, "Am I hurt or injured?" If you're going to win in life and marriage you must learn to play hurt.

I had a very interesting experience a few months ago while Jessi and I were doing a marriage event in Oahu. It's a terrible place to have to go but someone must teach marriage principles in Hawaii! We were doing a Q & A and the Pastor of the church asked me to talk about some of the tough times in life and marriage that we had to fight through. When did you have to play hurt as a couple? It kind of took me back for a second. I asked if the session was being recorded. I really didn't want to get that vulnerable on film, but I did it anyway. I began to recount the painful things that we made it through. Not alone but as a couple.

WE TOLD THE CROWD ABOUT:

1. My father dropped dead of a heart attack right in front of us just a few short weeks before my first child would be born. He was sixty-one and I was twenty-seven. We learned to play hurt.

2. Jessi's miscarriage of our second child. It was a real blow. It was also very public. That's the curse and the blessing of being a public figure. When tough things happen everyone wants to talk to you about it and it makes it hard to heal the wound. We learned to play hurt.

3. A very public and nasty divorce in our family. When things go wrong in ministry families, people show no mercy. They think Pastors and preachers should be perfect in every way. We watched everyone pick sides and go to war. We learned to play hurt.

4. At the same time this divorce happened in Jessi's family, my family hit a brick wall of legal problems. My father and his brother had built the largest cattle brokerage in America. When my father passed away, my mother sold her part of the company to his partner. Everything was fine until the 2008 stock market crash. The owner of the company was over-leveraged and began to take massive losses on beef and beef futures. To try to keep the loans coming, he cooked the books and created fake companies to move cattle back and forth so false sales could be reported. He was arrested and my family name was smeared in publications across America. Even Forbes wrote a nasty article. It hit the front page of the paper in the town I pastored and my family's integrity was called into question. My mother was innocent, my father had passed away before the incident but I had nothing to do with it. It didn't matter because legal battles were on. We learned to play hurt.

5. A nasty church split that we had to lead through. It happens to every church that's been in existence long enough. Just like the devil created a rebellion in heaven he is still trying to create rebellions in households, marriages, families, and even in churches. I don't know any significant leader that hasn't had to lead through accusations, betrayal, and the Judas kiss. Jessi and I had some people that we were very close to, and had done ministry with for a decade, turn on us. I questioned the ethics of some business practices

that they were getting involved in and in return they decided to try to destroy my character. They went to work calling everyone they could in the church, creating fellowship dinners that they hadn't created in years, with one goal in mind - Get Brian out! It was a painful time, friendships were lost, loyalties were tested, and even our children felt the sting. Living in a small community it became more than we expected. Jessi had to hire a babysitter if she wanted to go to the grocery in order to protect our children from the mean-spirited accusations and comments that people would hurl at her in public. We obviously didn't want other people's words and actions to affect our kids and their hearts towards people, church, and ultimately God. We learned to play hurt."

—Pastor Brian Gibson

HEAL TOGETHER

"WHEN THESE TOUGH TIMES HAPPEN IN LIFE YOU HAVE TO MAKE A DECISION AS A COUPLE THAT WE ARE GOING TO HEAL TOGETHER."

For some, it's very natural to retreat to a state of self-isolation during a time of great pain. Many people don't want others to see them hurt. It's where the old adage "tough guys don't cry" comes from. I want you to know, I cry and I consider myself a tough guy. When Andy went to college on Toy Story I was inconsolable (ha) God has given us the gift of marriage to help navigate the storms in life. Remember your spouse is someone you should run to in times of great pain, not someone you should run from.

During these times of pain, you do need to give each other great grace! Remember, this is only a season. The Bible says weeping will endure for a night but joy comes in the morning. During these times of pain we've learned to give each other a pass. Now that doesn't excuse every action, but it takes into account that you are hurting. People say things they don't mean when they're hurt. People do things they don't intend to do when they are hurt. None of us are exempt from this human behavior.

"I'll never forget one of the toughest times of my young adult life."

Jessi and I had been married and waited about six years before we started having children. Finally, Jessi became pregnant with our eldest daughter, Brileigh. We were so excited to be having a little girl. During this time my father called and asked if we would go on a vacation in Florida with him. I was super busy with a new church and didn't think I had time to fit it into my schedule. He prevailed through the voice of my mother and we ended up going with him.

We had a great trip. We ate like kings and played some of the greatest golf courses just north of West Palm Beach Florida. There was nothing we loved more than beating each other on the golf course. He won one day on the course and I won the next. After we were done golfing, the girls got ready and we all went out to eat. We had a great meal, we laughed and cut up at the restaurant. After the meal, we went back to the condo, and about an hour later I heard my mother scream. I ran into the room to find my father dying of a massive heart attack. I tried to do CPR, everyone in the house prayed, but we still lost him. It was a devastating loss. He was still young and strong.

After this loss I was more than just hurt, I was injured. It took time to get over this tragedy. Jessi had great grace on me and treated me with love. Although I hate to admit it, I allowed myself to slip into a semi-depression. I mourned the loss of my father for about two years. I allowed not just grief, but an attitude of grief to settle into my life. It's human and natural to grieve but just because one person has passed away doesn't mean that another person's life needs to end! The greatest gift that you can give to those who pass that you've loved is to really live your life to the max.

Jessi came to me after about two years of this and lovingly told me to shake it off. Enough was enough! She wanted to see me live life with joy again and she was right. It's one thing to grieve but it's another thing to let a spirit of grief settle into your life. Love helps us heal and handle the pain. Marriage provides a partner to help us see the blind spots in our lives. I'm so thankful that she loved me enough to say, it's time to move on. I believe that the two most important voices in our lives are the voice of God and the voice of our spouse. Let's use our voices to heal!"

–Pastor Brian Gibson

"I will never forget the day when we found out that the little baby we were expecting had a heart that stopped beating.

We had already announced to hundreds of people that we were expecting a baby and I was so excited. I wanted my kids to be very close in age and it wasn't going as fast as I had hoped so this baby was a big deal. When I came out of that regular checkup with terrible news I felt like I got sucker punched. My mind was racing."Maybe I didn't eat right." "Did I hurt the baby when I went on that plane?". Then my background of faith took over. Have you ever had your religion haunt you? I was so confused and in the deepest pain I had ever felt in my heart, I reached for the familiar. I was raised with a concept of "the open door". I still believe that this concept is real but to be honest I was not thinking straight. I was trying to explain away the loss of a child. I wanted to blame myself because it is easier for me than no answer. I began to ask Brian out loud. Where is the open door in our life that allowed this to happen?

What did I do to allow the enemy in? I was beating myself up. Brian looked at me with a very serious face and in a very loving tone he said, "Jessi, I will not allow you to do this to yourself. You are a good mom and you didn't DO anything. We live in a fallen world that looks like a crash site and we are experiencing that fallen world today. You did everything you knew to do and the baby didn't form fully. That has nothing to do with you and everything to do with the earth we live in." This was exactly what I needed. The pain of miscarriage was overwhelming. Brian released me from guilt and let me heal. The quickest and best way to heal hurt is in the presence of God. Shame keeps us out of it. We try to hide and beat up on ourselves. Brian exposed my hurt to the healing power of God by obliterating the shame. He called me back to a loving God and destroyed false narratives disguised as spiritual thoughts."

-Pastor Jessi Gibson

"THERE HAVE BEEN TIMES THAT JESSI WAS HELPING ME THROUGH MY PAIN AND THEN THERE HAVE BEEN TIMES THAT I WAS HELPING JESSI THROUGH HER PAIN!"

This is the joy of marriage – you have someone to help you through your suffering in a fallen world.

> "The LORD is near to those who have a
> broken heart, And saves such as have a
> contrite spirit."
> Psalms 34:18 NKJV

The ultimate one that heals us from hurt or serious injury is the Lord. The Bible reveals him as a healer! He loves to heal the broken, the broken in body, the broken in spirit, and the broken in heart. I believe that this verse from the Psalms shows us His method of healing the broken heart. I believe that the key verse is the word near. Whenever Jessi is really hurting she needs me to be near as a husband. Whenever I am really hurting I need Jessi to be near as a wife. I have to admit, there have been many times that I haven't been as near as I should have been. Those times are the ones I regret the most. I want to encourage you to make a fresh commitment to be near to your spouse when they're hurting, just like the Lord is near to us when we are hurting. I believe that love handles hurt!"

— Pastor Brian Gibson

LOVE HANDLE:

The next time you and/or your spouse experience hurt I want you to make a conscious decision to be near. Not obnoxiously hovering but near. When you are available you open the door for God to use you to bring and receive healing.

CHAPTER 10:

THE ULTIMATE LOVE HANDLE

"Greater love has no one than this,
than to lay down one's life for his
friends." John 15:13 NKJV

"THROUGH THE COURSE OF THIS BOOK, WE HAVE BEEN TALKING ABOUT LOVE HANDLES. THESE ARE THINGS YOU CAN GRAB HOLD OF IN LIFE."

Of all the things we hope you will grab ahold of, Jesus is number one because he has grabbed hold of eternal life for you. Jesus, at the cross, died for the sins of humanity and because of that death, you and I now have a choice to live. The life that God allows us to choose is the best life imaginable. You will never have a whole marriage unless you position Jesus in the middle of it.

Nothing in This broken world becomes whole without Jesus Christ of Nazareth. A marriage only becomes whole when it's based on Him. A person's true purpose is only found in Him. True life and eternity is only found in Him.

Jesus died on the cross. Crucifixion is a brutal death. He was beaten with a cat of nine tails at the whipping post before he went to the cross. Most men died at the whipping post. He was then nailed to the cross. He was nailed to the cross for our sins. The punishment for our sin was placed upon Him and He is our substitution on the cross.

The Bible records, after He died, He was placed in a tomb. On the third day, God resurrected Him. The scripture also promises that He is coming back!

If you would like to accept Christ as your Savior and place Him in the center of your marriage I want to encourage you to pray.

"Father, I'm a sinner. I need a Savior. I've lived my own way. I've done my own thing. I repent of my sin. I believe that Jesus is the son of God. I believe that He died for me. I believe He was placed in a tomb and on the third day resurrected. Come into my life. Save me, forgive me, fill me with the Holy Spirit. I boldly declare that Jesus is my Lord! Amen!"

—Pastor Brian Gibson

LOVE HANDLE:

Now that you have received Jesus, find a Bible believing Church to grow your faith in. Your marriage will work if you hold onto God and hold onto each other!!!!